George Clinton Gilmore

Manchester Men

Soldiers and Sailors in the Civil War

George Clinton Gilmore

Manchester Men
Soldiers and Sailors in the Civil War

ISBN/EAN: 9783337135188

Printed in Europe, USA, Canada, Australia, Japan

Cover: Foto ©ninafisch / pixelio.de

More available books at **www.hansebooks.com**

GEN. RICHARD N. BATCHELDER.

Quartermaster 1st N. H. Vols., April 29, '61; Capt. A. Q. M., U. S. Vols., Aug. 3, '61; Lt. Col., Chief Quartermaster 2d Army Corps, Jan. 1, '63; Col., Chief Quartermaster Army of the Potomac, June 18, '64; Capt. A. Q. M.,
U. S. Army, Feb. 16, '65; Maj. Q. M., Jan. 18, '67; Lt. Col., Deputy Q. M. Gen., Mar. 10, '82; Brig. Gen., Quartermaster General U. S. Army, June 26, '90; Bvt. Maj., Lt. Col., Col., and Brig. Gen., U. S. V., Bvt. Maj., Lt. Col.,
and Col., U. S. Army, for faithful and meritorious service during the war; Medal of Honor for distinguished
gallantry Oct. 13-15, '63.

MANCHESTER MEN.

SOLDIERS AND SAILORS

IN THE

CIVIL WAR, 1861-'66.

BY

GEORGE C. GILMORE.

CONCORD, N. H.:
THE RUMFORD PRESS
1898.

Paid a commendable tribute to the memory of the brave men, living or dead, who represented the State in the Civil War, by appropriating thirty-two thousand, four hundred dollars, to prepare and print two thousand volumes of the " Revised Register of the Soldiers and Sailors of New Hampshire in the War of the Rebellion, 1861-'66, Prepared and Published by Authority of the Legislature, by Augustus D. Ayling, Adjutant-General."

One city and several towns have published the record containing the names of the men who represented them. The main object in the publication of this small book, too long delayed since the close of the war, is to furnish the people of Manchester with an alphabetically arranged record, copied from General Ayling's Register, for easy reference to the pages as indicated, for all the particulars regarding the men who represented this city in the Civil War.

GEORGE C. GILMORE.

Manchester, N. H., August 12, 1898.

CITY GOVERNMENT, 1861.

MAYOR.
DAVID A. BUNTON.

ALDERMEN.

Ward 1—GILMORE, GEORGE C.
Ward 2—TEBBETTS, JAMES A.
Ward 3—MERRILL, HENRY C.
Ward 4—BEAN, JAMES M.*
        MAYNARD, JOHN H.
Ward 5—COUGHLIN, JOHN
Ward 6—HAYNES, ELBRIDGE G.
Ward 7—SMITH, JOHN C.
Ward 8—MONTGOMERY, THOMAS S.

COUNCILMEN.

Ward 1—CAMPBELL, HENRY A.
        WOODMAN, ELBRIDGE G.
        PULSIFER, JEREMIAH O.
Ward 2—CRAM, GEORGE T.
        HACKETT, JOSIAH
        CLEMENT, CHARLES W.
Ward 3—GOODALE, JOHN H.
        BARKER, ALBION
        PEABODY, EPHRAIM S.

---

* Died January 26. John H. Maynard elected to fill vacancy.

Ward 4—MILLIKEN, SETH
FRENCH, EBEN
PALMER, WILLIAM S.
Ward 5—BURNS, HUGH
CONNER, DANIEL
GILLIS, JOHN
Ward 6—KIMBALL, EZRA
KENDALL, BENJAMIN C.
ADAMS, CHARLES W.
Ward 7—MACK, DANIEL
RAND, JOHN H.
HARTSHORN, ELBRIDGE
Ward 8—CASSIDY, DENNIS
WARREN, EDWIN R.
TODD, WILLIAM

[DAILY MIRROR—EXTRA.]

SATURDAY, APRIL 13, 1861.

WAR BEGUN.

Sumter Attacked!

[Special Dispatch to the Daily Mirror.]

BOSTON, Apr. 13.

Fighting commenced at Charleston yesterday. Seven batteries played on Sumter all day, and Anderson replied. Rumored, portions of the Fort destroyed. Two Confederate troops wounded. Bombardment be resumed to-day.

LATER.

CHARLESTON, April 12. War is inaugurated. The batteries on Sullivan's Island, Morris Island, at other points opened on Ft. Sumter at 4 o'clock this morning. Fort Sumter has returned the fire and a brisk cannonading has been kept up—no information has been received from the seaboard yet. The military are under arms and the whole populace on the street.

STILL LATER.

The firing has continued all day uninterruptedly. Two of the Ft. Sumter guns have been silenced, and it is reported that a breach has been made in the south-east wall. The answer to Gen. Beauregard's demand by Maj. Anderson was that he would surrender when his supplies were exhausted, if he was not reinforced.

Not a casualty has yet happened to any of the force of 19 batteries—only 7 had yet been opened on Sumter. The remainder are held in reserve for the expected fleet.—2000 men reached the city this morning and embarked for Morris Island.

The firing has ceased for the night to be resumed at daylight in the morning, unless an attempt is made to reinforce Fort Sumter, to repel which ample arrangements have been made. Only two men were wounded to-day.

The Pawnee, Harriet Lane and another steamer are reported off the bar. April 13, 12:30. It is impossible to reinforce Fort Sumter to-night as a storm is raging. The mortar battery will be playing on Fort Sumter all night.

PRESIDENT LINCOLN'S CALLS FOR TROOPS DURING THE CIVIL WAR.

	Number of Men.	N. H. Quota.	Fur- nished.	Time.
Call of April 15, 1861..	75,000	780	779	3 months.
Call of May 3, 1861....	500,000	9,234	8,338	3 years.
Call of July 2, 1862....	300,000	5,053	6,390	3 years.
Call of Aug. 4, 1862....	300,000	5,053	1,736	9 months.
Call of Oct. 17, 1863*} Call of Feb. 1, 1864..}	500,000	6,469	*6,974	3 years.
Call of March 14, 1864†	200,000	2,558	†2,965	3 years.
Call of July 18, 1864‡..	500,000	4,648	‡5,973	1, 2, 3 years.
Call of Dec. 19, 1864§..	300,000	2,072	§1,304	1, 2, 3, 4 yrs.
Militia, for 100 days...	....	....	167	....
Totals...........	2,675,000	35,867	34,629	

Reduced to a three years standard................. 30,849
In the navy and marine corps............................ 3,526
Number of men who served in other states............ 1,883

It is found impossible to obtain definite information as to the number of men required of the city of Manchester, under the several calls, or the credits given, as will be seen by the subjoined correspondence:

WASHINGTON, June 11, 1898.

MY DEAR MR. GILMORE:—I send you all that it has been possible to get from the War Department, in answer to the request contained in your favor of the 6th instant.

Sincerely yours,

J. H. GALLINGER.

Hon. George C. Gilmore,
Manchester, N. H.

---

*Including 571 who paid commutation. † Including 121 who paid commutation. Total, 629.

‡ For 1 year, 1,921; 2 years, 25; 3 years, 4,027.

§ For 1 year, 492; 2 years, 9; 3 years, 775; 4 years, 28.

Quotas of Manchester, N. H., War of the Rebellion.

RECORD AND PENSION OFFICE,

WAR DEPARTMENT,

WASHINGTON CITY,

June 10, 1898.

Hon. J. H. Gallinger, United States Senate :—

SIR:—In returning herewith the letter of your correspondent, Mr. George C. Gilmore of Manchester, New Hampshire, received yesterday with your letter of the 8th instant, and in response to Mr. Gilmore's request for information as to the quotas of the City of Manchester under the several calls for troops during the War of the Rebellion, I am directed by the Secretary of War, to advise you as follows:

No record of the quota of the City of Manchester was kept for any call for troops prior to that of February 1, 1864. For that call and subsequent calls, the quotas of Manchester are shown by the records to have been as follows:

Sub. Dist.	Ward.	Quota.				Totals.
		Under call of 1864.				
		Feb. 1	March 14	July 18	Dec. 19	
47	1	54	22	60	11	147
48	2	45	18	50	..	113
49	3	65	24	72	10	171
50	4	66	25	69	2	162
51	5	32	13	62	..	107
52	6	50	20	53	12	135
53	7	21	8	22	7	58
54	8	9	4	10	3	26
Totals..........		342	134	398	45	919

It is shown by the records that the quotas for the State of New Hampshire under the calls of 1861 and 1862, were as follows:

Under calls of 1861	9,234
Under call of July 2, 1862, for 300,000 volunteers,	5,053
Under call of August 4, 1862, for 300,000 militia,	5,053

Very respectfully,

F. C. AINSWORTH,

Colonel, U. S. Army, Chief,

Record and Pension Officer.

ABBOTT GUARDS.

"Upon the first call for troops, April 15, 1861, the men were enlisted for three months by Frederick Smyth, and on the 24th of April went to Concord to join the First regiment, being the first company to report at that place." See page 1,194 of Gen. Ayling's Revised Register.

The Abbott Guards were from Manchester.

The following is a list of the members of the Abbott Guard who were yesterday enlisted into the service of the State by Hon. Fred. Smyth, recruiting officer, appointed for the purpose by Adj. Gen. Abbott. The whole number is 74; every man with the exception of one—who gives a decisive answer this morning—came forward at roll-call and took the oath. The drummer and fifer are not yet enlisted. The whole number of men in the company is 77; 3 commissioned, and 8 non-commissioned officers; 2 musicians and 64 privates. The * signifies those who are married.

Members.	Age.	Occupation.
Wm. C. Knowlton,* Capt.,	38	Machinist.
Edw. L. Bailey, 1st Lieut.,	19	Clerk.
Jos. A. Hubbard,* 2d Lieut.,	28	Machinist.
Geo. W. Gordon,* O'd'ly Serg't,	27	Machinist.
David M. Perkins,* 2d Serg't,	29	Butcher.
Rodney A. Manning, 3d Serg't,	22	Machinist.

Members.	Age.	Occupation.
Chs. E. Palmer,* 4th Serg't,	21	Machinist.
Wm. H. D. Cochrane, Clerk,	22	Student.
Thorndike P. Heath,*	28	Teamster.
Oscar A. Mooar,	21	Mechanic.
Edgar D. Kenaston,	21	Carpenter.
Charles Vickery,	20	Machinist.
Frank M. Boutelle,	18	Clerk.
Perkins C. Lane,	21	Carpenter.
James M. House,	20	Machinist.
Moses A. Hunkins,*	33	Shoemaker.
George F. Lawrence,*	33	Carpenter.
Chas. T. Hardy,	19	Carpenter.
John Whitten,	28	Farmer.
James G. Burns,	20	Iron Founder.
Chas. B. Wright,	19	Machinist.
Martin A. Haynes,	19	Printer.
Henry M. Pillsbury,*	27	Mechanic.
Hazen B. Martin,*	27	Iron Founder.
Josiah S. Swain,	20	Farmer.
Luther P. Hubbard, Jr.,	21	Mechanic.
Geo. C. Johnston,	21	Carpenter.
Joseph H. Gleason,	21	Teamster.
Lyman A. Dickey,	21	Blacksmith.
Moses L. Eastman,	23	Machinist.
Julius L. Beede,	24	Farmer.
Geo. B. Damon,	26	Barber.
James R. Carr,	20	Painter.
John E. Ogden,	24	Mechanic.
Lewis G. Clock,	24	Machinist.
Frank C. Wasley,	21	Painter.
John S. Colley,	25	Mechanic.
Albert B. Robinson,	19	Tanner.
Wm. H. Appleton,	19	Machinist.
Levi H. Sleeper, Jr.,	23	Iron Founder.
Leonard B. Corliss,	19	Mechanic.
Wm. Welles Wood,	19	Teamster.
Solon F. Porter,	22	Mechanic.
Samuel H. Oliver,	23	Mechanic.

Members.	Age.	Occupation.
Lyman B. Sleeper,	35	Machinist.
Stephen Dearborn,*	26	Farmer.
Chas. H. Smiley,	20	Iron Founder.
Geo. A. Clark,*	23	Mechanic.
Geo. W. Vickery,	22	Currier.
Wm. N. Philbrook,	19	Mechanic.
Chas. D. Moulton,*	25	Mechanic.
Wm. B. Adams,	23	Mechanic.
Clifford K. Burns,	23	Mechanic.
Benj. D. Belcher,	25	Mechanic.
James O. Chandler,	24	Painter.
Willard P. Thompson,*	28	Mechanic.
Eugene G. Hazewell.	18	Printer.
Albert Story,	23	Mechanic.
Stephen J. Smiley,	34	Iron Founder.
Edwin Stark,	22	Mechanic.
Chester C. Smith,*	26	Mechanic.
Geo. W. Clay,	23	Shoemaker.
Geo. H. Johnson,	27	Shoemaker.
Jas. S. Gilmore,	25	Machinist.
Stephen S. Fifield,*	24	Mechanic.
Jerome C. Dow,	18	Mechanic.
Nathaniel Southard,	22	Printer.
Jesse E. Dewey,	18	Mechanic·
Solomon M. Smith,	20	Mechanic.
James P. Dunn,	22	Mechanic.
Nicholas M. Biglin,	22	Mechanic.
Fernando C. Spaulding,*	24	Paper Maker.
Benj. L. Hartshorn,	21	Paper Maker.
John Brown,	19	Mechanic.

The number of Soldiers and Sailors from New Hampshire, who served in the Civil war:

New Hampshire Organizations,	32,486
Veteran Reserve Corps,	413
United States Colored Troops,	396
United States Army,	156
United States Volunteers,	71

United States Veteran Volunteers,	12
United States Navy,	3,160
United States Marine Corps,	366
Citizens or residents of New Hampshire, who served in other states,	1,883
Total,	38,943

See Gen. Ayling's Record, page 1,223.

Population of the United States in 1860,	31,445,080
Population of New Hampshire in 1860,	326,172
Population of Manchester in 1860,	20,107

Number males, 8,668; females, 11,439.

Amount of money paid in bounties by Manchester, to 1,483 men, Soldiers and Sailors. See City Reports, 1862–'66:

Soldier's Bounty, paid 1862,	$17,350.00
Soldier's Bounty, paid 1863,	141,913.52
Soldier's Bounty, paid 1864,	87,150.00
Soldier's Bounty, paid 1865,	66,081.12
Soldier's Bounty, paid 1866,	129.72
Total,	$312,624.36

Amount of money paid the families of Soldiers and Sailors, with the names and amount each received. See City Reports.

1861, page 121,	$14,253.75
1862, page 93,	61,451.00
1863, page 106,	52,877.12
1864, page 105,	46,443.48
1865, page 116,	23,801.60
1866, page 24,	67.23
Total,	$198,894.18

SUMMARY.

Number of men from Manchester, including substitutes and non-residents credited,	2,687
Manchester men who enlisted in other states and for cities and towns in this state,	194
Making a total of,	2,881

Manchester in 1860, according to population, was 16 22-100 part of the state. On that basis, her proportion of Soldiers and Sailors would have been, 2,401

Residence of the men, who enlisted prior to July 2, 1862, as given in the enlistment rolls, very uncertain as to their actual residence.

Average bounty to the 1,483 men paid by the city, \$210.81

Number of Manchester men killed, 86

Number of Manchester men who died of wounds, 59

Number of Manchester men who died of disease, 188

Number of Manchester men wounded, 412

Number of Manchester men deserted, 327

Of this number, 137 were substitutes.

Dishonorably discharged, 10

*Executed for desertion, 2

ABBREVIATIONS.

1 V. C. First Regiment New England Volunteer Cavalry.

1 V. C. First Regiment New Hampshire Volunteer Cavalry.

1 L. B. First New Hampshire Light Battery.

1 H. A. First Company New Hampshire Volunteer Heavy Artillery.

1 H. A. First Regiment New Hampshire Volunteer Heavy Artillery.

1 R. S. First Regiment United States Volunteer Sharpshooters.

2 R. S. Second Regiment United States Volunteer Sharpshooters.

N. G. National Guards, New Hampshire Volunteer Infantry.

M. G. Martin Guards, New Hampshire Volunteer Infantry.

V. R. C. Veteran Reserve Corps.

C. T. United States Colored Troops.

D. C. Dartmouth Cavalry.

SOUVENIR.

LAST FOURTEEN SURVIVORS

OF THE

REVOLUTIONARY ARMY.

AMAZIAH GOODWIN.

Born in Somersworth, New Hampshire, February 16, 1759; resided in Alfred, Maine; died in Dover, New Hampshire, June 22, 1863, aged 104 years, 4 months, 7 days.

BENJAMIN MILLER.

Born in Springfield, Massachusetts, April 4, 1764; died ———— September 24, 1863, aged 99 years, 5 months, 21 days.

JOHN GOODNOW.

Born in Sudbury, Massachusetts, January 30, 1762; died ———— October 22, 1863, aged 101 years, 8 months, 23 days.

JONAS GATES.

Born ———— July 7, 1764; died in Chelsea, Vermont, January 14, 1864, aged 99 years, 6 months, 8 days.

JOHN PETTINGILL.

Born in Windham, Connecticut, November 30, 1764; died in Henderson, New York, April 23, 1864, aged 99 years, 4 months, 24 days.

REV. DANIEL WALDO.

Born in Windham, Scotland Parish, Connecticut, September 10, 1762; resided at Syracuse, New York; graduated at Yale College in 1778; elected chaplain of the House of

Representatives of the United States December 22, 1856, and reëlected for a second term; died —— July 30, 1864, aged 101 years, 10 months, 21 days.

ADAM LINK.

Born in Washington county, Pennsylvania, near Hagerstown, Maryland, November 14, 1761; died at Sulphur Springs, Crawford county, Ohio, August 15, 1864, aged 102 years, 9 months, 2 days.

ALEXANDER MILLENER.

Born in Quebec, Canada, March 14, 1760; died at Adams Basin, New York, March 13, 1865, aged 105 years. He enlisted under the name of Alexander Maroney, his widowed mother having married a man of that name. Buried in Mount Hope cemetery, Rochester, New York.

JAMES BARHAM.

Born in Southampton county, Virginia, May 18, 1764; died in Green county, Missouri, July 18, (?) 1865, aged 101 years, 2 months, 1 day.

WILLIAM HUTCHINGS.

Born in York, York county, Maine, October 6, 1764; resided in Penobscot, Hancock county, Maine; died May 2, 1866, aged 101 years, 6 months, 27 days.

LEMUEL COOK.

Born in Northbury, Litchfield county, Connecticut, September 10, 1759; resided in Clarendon, New York; died May 20, 1866, aged 106 years, 8 months, 11 days.

SAMUEL DOWNING.

Born in Newburyport, Massachusetts, November 30, 1761; resided in Deering, New Hampshire; died in Edinburg, New York, February 19, 1867, aged 105 years, 2 months, 20 days.

JOHN GRAY.

Born near Mount Vernon, Virginia, January 6, 1764; died near Hiramsburg, Ohio, March 29, 1868, aged 104 years, 2 months, 24 days; pensioned by special act of Congress.

DANIEL FREDERICK BOCHMAN.

[Bakeman on muster and pay-rolls.]

Born in Schoharie county, New York, September 28, 1759 ; died in Freedom, Cattaraugus county, New York, April 5, 1869, aged 109 years, 6 months, 8 days ; pensioned by special act of Congress.

REVOLUTIONARY WAR.

According to Haydn's Dictionary of Dates, the Revolutionary war commenced July 14, 1774, and the treaty of peace signed September 3, 1783. The Continental army was disbanded at Newburg, New York, November 3, 1783, and the treaty of peace ratified by Congress, January 4, 1784.

WAR OF 1812.

War with Great Britain was declared by the United States June 18, 1812; the treaty of peace signed December 24, 1814, and ratified February 17, 1815.

WAR WITH MEXICO.

Mexico declared war against the United States June 4, 1845 ; the treaty of peace was ratified May 19, 1848.

WAR OF THE REBELLION.

Commenced April 12, 1861. The President proclaimed the insurrection at an end April 3, 1866, except in Texas, and there August 20, 1866.

Daniel Frederick Bochman lived 85 years, 3 months, and 1 day after the close of the Revolutionary war.

A soldier of the War of 1812, living the same length of time after the close of the war, would live until May 18, 1900 ; a Mexican war soldier, until August 20, 1933 ; a soldier of the Rebellion, until August 3, 1951.

PENSION ROLLS.

In 1820, the United States government printed one volume, and, in 1835–'36, three more, said to contain the names of 120,000 pensioners who were soldiers in the Revolution. The names are grouped by counties in the respective states, and the tables show dates of pensions, branch of service, age, amount of money paid to each up to March 4, 1834, and dates of death of perhaps one fourth of those who had died. The number of New Hampshire pensioners named in the four volumes is 2,906.

In June, 1840, a census of pensioners was taken throughout the country, and the names, ages, and places of residence of over 21,000 pensioners were obtained, of which number, 1,412 were New Hampshire soldiers. This roll was published in a separate volume by the government.

The applications of New Hampshire soldiers for pensions, state places of residence as follows: in New Hampshire, 1,558; Maine, 333; Massachusetts, 95; Vermont, 448; Canada, 30; Connecticut, 17; New York, 289; Ohio, 73; Pennsylvania, 28; Kentucky, 7; New Jersey, 3; Michigan, 10; Indiana, 7; Illinois, 3; Virginia, Maryland, Georgia, and the District of Columbia, 1 each.

GEORGE C. GILMORE.

MANCHESTER, N. H., September 25, 1897.

SOLDIERS' MONUMENT, MERRIMACK SQUARE.
DEDICATED SEPTEMBER 11, 1879.

MANCHESTER MEN IN THE CIVIL WAR.

Copied from the "Revised Register of the Soldiers and Sailors of New Hampshire in the War of the Rebellion, 1861–1866," Prepared and Published by Authority of the Legislature, by Augustus D. Ayling, Adjutant-General.

MANCHESTER MEN IN THE CIVIL WAR.

Names.	Reg.	Page.	Remarks.
Abbott, Charles H.	7	355	
Abbott, Daniel B.	10	517	Deserted.
Abbott, Edward P.	1 V. C.	832	Wounded.
Abbott, Joseph C.	7	355	
Abbott, Joseph S.	8	409	Deserted.
Abbott, Ira S.	9	461	
Abbott, Michael	15	737	
Abbott, Selwin B.	10	517	
Abbott, Wiggin T.	M. G.	995	
Adams, Charles A.	7	355	
Adams, Charles A.	7	355	
Adams, Eben	3	102	Wounded.
Adams, Edward	11	557	Wounded.
Adams, Ira J.	3	102	Died Wds., July 2, '64,
Adams, John	2	29	
Adams, Thomas	2	29	Deserted.
Adams, Thomas J.	7	1028	(7) Rhode Island. Wd.
Agnew, James	12	607	
Ahern, John	10	517	
Aims, Clement F. S.	7	355	
Aldrich, John C.	1	3	
Aldrich, John C.	8	410	
Aldrich, John C.*	8	410	Killed March 27, '65.
Aldrich, Lyman M.	2	30	
Aldrich, Miles	10	517	Died Wds.,June 29, '64.
Aldrich, Henry H.	1 V. C.	853	
Allen, Charles H.	1	3	
Allen, Charles H.	4	157	
Allen, Frederick R.	2	30	
Allen, George	3	103	Wounded.
Allen, Robert H.	3	103	Wounded.
Allen, William	3	103	
Allen, Francis A.	4	157	
Allen, Francis A.	4	157	Wounded.
Allen, James M.	4	157	Died Nov. 25, '61.
Allen, John	7	356	Wounded. Deserted.
Allen, George W.	8	410	Deserted.
Allen, Isaac	8	410	Deserted.
Allen, Daniel	10	517	
Allen, William H.	10	517	Died July 6, '63.

* By a citizen of Natchez, Miss.

◆

MANCHESTER MEN IN THE CIVIL WAR—*Continued.*

NAMES.	Reg.	Page.	Remarks.
Allen, Jeremiah C.	10	517	Died July 27, '63.
Allen, John L.	1 H. A.	921	
Alexander, Julius	2	30	Deserted.
Alexander, Emery W.	N. G.	992	
Altland, George	12	607	
Ambuda, A. O.	10	518	Died Jan. 5, '63.
Ames, George H.	1 H. A.	922	
Andrews, Charles J.	1	3	
Andrews, Charles J.	3	103	Deserted.
Anderson, James	4	157	
Anderson, James	10	518	
Anderson, Hans	12	607	
Angell, Jesse F.	10	518	Wounded.
Annis, Zebina N.	4	157	
Annis, Zebina N.	4	157	Wounded.
Annis, Augustus C.	8	410	
Annis, Augustus C.	8	410	Died Wds., May 20,' 64.
Antlitz, John	9	432	Wounded.
Applebee, George	1 H. A.	922	
Appleton, William H.	2	31	
Appleton, William H.	C. T.	1016	
Appleton, James	7	356	Deserted.
Armstrong, Andrew	N. G.	992	
Arnold, James	11	558	Died Feb. 16, '64.
Arnold, Joseph	14	1029	(14) Mass.
Ash, Lewis	7	356	Deserted.
Ashton, George E.	Navy.	1098	
Atherton, James W.	1	3	
Atherton, James W.	1 V. C.	832	
Atherton, James W.	1 H. A.	922	
Atherton, James W.	Navy.	1098	
Atkins, George	1 R. C.	854	Deserted.
Atwood, Charles W.	10	518	
Atwood, Daniel	10	518	
Atwood, Daniel N.	3	103	Wounded.
Austin, William H. H.	4	158	Wounded.
Austin, William H. H.	V.R.C.	1004	
Austin, John H.	8	410	
Austin, John H.	8	410	
Austin, Joseph A.	1 V. C.	832	

MANCHESTER MEN IN THE CIVIL WAR—*Continued.*

Names.	Reg.	Page.	Remarks.
Ayer, Henry G.	1 V. C.	832	
Babbet, William L.	1 L. B.	897	Killed Aug. 29, '62.
Bacon, Francis D.	2	31	
Bacon, Ebenezer	28	1030	(28) Mass. Wounded.
Bagley, Jonathan R.	4	158	
Bagley, Samuel	5	214	Died Wds., July 10, '65.
Bailey, Edward L.	2	51	Wounded.
Bailey, Edward L.	4	1030	(4) Inft., U. S. A.
Bailey, George	3	103	Wounded.
Bailey, Rufus	4	158	
Bailey, Joseph W.	4	158	Died Aug. 4, '62.
Bailey, Henry A.	10	518	Wounded.
Bailey, Joseph	10	518	Wounded.
Bailey, Charles L.	1 H. A.	922	
Bailey, Charles L.	M. G.	995	
Baird, John	1 V. C.	854	Deserted.
Baker, John H.	4	158	
Baker, James B. T.	10	518	
Baker, Stephen M.	10	518	Died Dec. 29, '62.
Baker, Washington I.	10	518	Killed Dec. 13, '62.
Baker, Charles N.	11	558	
Baker, Edwin N.	1 L. B.	897	
Baker, Elbridge G.	1 H. A.	922	
Baker, Elihu B.	N. G.	992	
Baker, Willard S.	1 H. A.	922	
Baker, William	3	104	Wounded.
Ballou, James H.	8	411	Died Feb. 4, '62.
Ballou, George W.	N. G.	992	
Balch, John C.	10	518	
Baldwin, James J.	10	518	
Banfill, Haskell W.	3	104	
Barker, John A.	2	32	Wounded.
Barker, William S.	4	158	
Barker, William S.	4	158	
Barrett, John	3	104	Killed July 10, '63.
Barrett, Edward R.	6	289	Died March 24, '64.
Barrett, William A.	10	518	Killed Dec. 13, '62.
Barr, Albert T.	18	804	
Barr, Albert T.	N. G.	992	
Bartels, Jacob	3	104	Died Nov. 12, '61.

MANCHESTER MEN IN THE CIVIL WAR—*Continued.*

NAMES.	Reg.	Page.	Remarks.
Barry, John	10	519	Deserted.
Barton, William	11	559	Deserted.
Barnes, Walter	5	214	
Barnes, Hiram S.	10	519	Died Wds., May 24, '64.
Barnard, Robert	12	609	Deserted.
Barney, Alanson W.	4	158	
Barney, Alanson W.	4	158	Killed May 15, '64.
Bartlett, Ezra S.	1	4	
Bartlett, Ezra S.	8	411	Killed June 14, '63.
Bartlett, Charles H.	4	158	Died Oct. 5, '62.
Bartlett, Ichabod S.	10	519	
Bartlett, Wilson A.	10	519	
Battles, Henry W.	7	357	Died July 26, '62.
Batchelder, Richard N.	1	4	
Batchelder, Richard N.	U.S.A.	1031	
Batchelder, Charles L.	4	159	
Batchelder, Charles L.	7	357	
Batchelder, John	2	32	
Batchelder, Henry S.	7	357	
Batchelder, Joseph W.	10	519	
Batchelder, Warren	10	519	Died Nov. 22, '62.
Batchelder, Leroy S.	N. G.	992	
Bauman, Victor	12	609	Deserted.
Bean, Leroy T.	1	4	
Bean, Leroy T.	1 L. B.	897	
Bean, Leroy T.	1 L. B.	897	Wounded.
Bean, John R.	1 L. B	897	
Bean, Lyman W.	1 L. B.	897	
Bean, Lyman W.*	1 L. B.	897	Died June 8, '64.
Bean, Charles	1 H. A.	923	
Bean, George W.	7	357	
Bean, George W.	7	357	
Bean, Amos S.	9	986	
Bean, George E.	10	519	Killed June 3, '64.
Bean, Watson	8	411	
Bean, James M.	1 V. C.	855	
Beaman, Charles F.	7	357	Died Wds., July 26, '63.
Beaman, Eri B.	7	357	
Beaty, Thomas	2	33	Deserted.
Beckwith, Oliver P.	1 L. B.	897	Died Aug. 15, '62.

* From injuries in the army.

MANCHESTER MEN IN THE CIVIL WAR—*Continued.*

NAMES.	Reg.	Page.	Remarks.
Bell, Robert	12	609	Deserted.
Bellice, Alexander	2	33	
Bennett, William S.	2	33	
Bennett, William L.	3	104	
Bennett, Henry	1 H. A.	923	
Beneresscheia, Jop C.	2	33	Wounded. Deserted.
Berham, Alfred W.	2	33	Wounded.
Berry, John	4	159	
Berry, George W.	1 V. C.	833	
Bess, Joseph	C. T.	1017	
Best, Gustavus H.	1 V. C.	855	
Biglin, Nicholas M.	2	33	Died June 24, '64.
Bickford, Horatio N.	4	159	
Bickford, Horatio N.	4	159	
Bickford, Jackson C.	18	804	
Bills, Charles W.	18	804	
Bixby, Avery	7	358	
Bixby, Avery	7	358	
Bixby, Newell R.	7	358	Wounded.
Black, William H. H.	1	4	
Blackburn, William H.	1 L. B.	897	
Blain, Joseph C.	10	519	
Blair, Henry	1 H. A.	924	
Blaisdell, Jerome	1	4	
Blaisdell, Jerome	4	160	
Blaisdell, George	2	33	Deserted.
Blake, James W.	2	34	
Blake, Lauson	3	105	
Blake, George G.	8	412	
Blake, George G.	8	412	
Blake, Thomas	8	412	
Blanchard, Franklin F.	7	358	Died Sept. 16, '62.
Blanchett, Joseph	7	358	
Blanchett, Joseph	7	358	Deserted.
Blood, Albert	3	105	
Blood, Albert	V.R.C.	1005	
Blood, Samuel L.	11	1033	(11) Mass. Wounded.
Bly, Jerry W.	8	412	Killed May 31, '63.
Bohan, Patrick	1	4	
Bohan, Patrick	8	412	Died Aug. 13, '62.

Names.	Reg.	Page.	Remarks.
Bond, Edson	9	986	
Bond, Henry E.	1 L. B.	897	
Bonner, William	4	160	
Bonner, Charles	10	519	
Bonynge, Thomas	1 V. C.	833	
Booth, John	3	105	Died Wds., June 16, '62.
Bourrell, Henry	1	4	
Boutelle, Frank M.	2	34	
Boutelle, Frank M.	N. G.	992	
Boutelle, George B.	1 H. A.	924	
Boutelle, George B.	N. G.	992	
Boutelle, William E.	1 H. A.	925	
Boutelle, William E.	N. G.	992	
Bowen, Ira A.	8	412	
Bowers, Charles	12	610	Deserted.
Bowker, Andrew M.	1 H. A.	925	
Bowker, Andrew M.	N. G.	992	Died Nov. 10, '65.
Bowker, James A.	1 H. A.	925	
Bowman, Eugene M.	1 V. C.	833	
Bowman, Eli E.	3	106	Wd. Died Mar. 10, '65.
Boyd, Charles W.	1 L. B.	897	
Boyd, Charles W.	1 L. B.	897	
Boyd, Henry C.	13	1033	(13 H. A.) New York.
Boyle, James	10	520	
Boyle, James	V.R.C.	1005	
Boynton, Francis	3	106	Wounded.
Brackett, Franklin A.	1 H. A.	925	
Brackett, Franklin A.	M. G.	995	
Bradley, Charles B.	N. G.	992	[Dec. 23, '64.
Bradley, George*	5	217	Deserted. Executed
Bradley, John	8	412	Deserted.
Bradbury, John W.	7	358	
Bradford, Charles H.	M. G.	995	
Brandon, Philip	7	358	
Branson, George	C. T.	1017	
Brelsford, Samuel D.	3	106	
Brelsford, Samuel D.	3	106	Wounded.
Bresnahan, Michael	4	160	
Bresnahan, Michael	4	160	
Bresnahan, Dennis	19	1034	(19) Mass.

* Bradley was a substitute.

33

MANCHESTER MEN IN THE CIVIL WAR — *Continued.*

Names.	Reg.	Page.	Remarks.
Breen, Timothy	8	412	
Bremier, Tobias C.	8	412	
Brennan, Thomas	8	412	
Brian, James O.	1 H. A.	925	
Briant, David	3	106	
Briant, David	3	106	Wounded.
Brickett, Charles A.	10	520	
Brickett, George T.	Navy.	1102	
Bridgham, George W.	3	106	Died Oct. 19, '62.
Brigham, Ephraim T.	4	160	Deserted.
Briggs, George H.	3	196	
Briggs, America	3	106	Killed May 18, '64.
Broderick, Patrick	4	161	
Broderick, Patrick	4	161	
Broderick, Michael	8	413	Wounded.
Brooks, William H.	4	161	
Brooks, William H.	4	161	Wd. Died Nov. 14, '64.
Brosnan, Patrick	8	413	
Brown, Abraham	1	5	
Brown, Abraham	1 R. A.	1034	(1 R. A.) Rhode Island.
Brown, Abraham	13	1034	(13) Mass.
Brown, Alfred	5	218	Deserted.
Brown, Allen W.	1 V. C.	856	Deserted.
Brown, Alexander	4	161	
Brown, Alexander A.	1 L. B.	897	
Brown, Asa	9	986	Died July 18, '63.
Brown, Augustus S.	1	5	Died Feb. 14, '62.
Brown, Calvin	7	359	Wounded.
Brown, Charles A.	1 V. C.	856	
Brown, Charles L.	1	5	
Brown, Charles L.	4	161	Died June 3, '63.
Brown, Charles W.	2	35	Deserted.
Brown, David	2	35	Wounded.
Brown, Edward	12	611	
Brown, Edward	58	1034	(58) Mass.
Brown, Edward F.	1 V. C.	856	
Brown, Francis	1 H. A.	925	
Brown, George W.	15	740	
Brown, George W.	1 H. A.	925	
Brown, James	4	161	Deserted.

MANCHESTER MEN IN THE CIVIL WAR—*Continued.*

Names.	Reg.	Page.	Remarks.
Brown, James S.	34	1034	(34) Mass.
Brown, James W.	Navy.	1104	Deserted.
Brown, Martin L.	1 H. A.	926	
Brown, William O. H.	3	107	Killed July 18, '63.
Brown, William	2	36	
Brown, William	2	36	Deserted.
Brown, William E.	8	413	
Brown, William E.	8	413	
Brown, William G.	7	360	Died July 11, '65.
Brown, William W.	7	360	
Brown, Warren E. F.	7	359	Killed July 18, '63.
Brown, Thomas	5	219	
Bruce, John N.	14	700	Wounded.
Bruce, John R.	14	700	
Brule, Auguste.	8	413	Deserted.
Brunke, Henri	2	36	Wounded.
Bryant, Orlando C.	2	1035	(2) Kentucky.
Bryson, John	10	520	Wounded.
Buckminster, Arthur E.	2	36	
Buckminster, Arthur E.	2	36	
Buckminster, Alvah	9	467	Killed May 12, '64.
Buckminster, James	N. G.	992	
Buckminster, William	1 H. A.	926	
Buckminster, William	N. G.	992	
Buckland, Lucius L.	11	562	
Buckley, Timothy	Navy.	1104	
Buckman, Charles N.	3	107	
Bullen, George	2	36	
Bully, Peter	18	806	
Bumford, James A.	11	562	
Bunce, Peter	1 H. A.	926	
Bundy, Marcus H.	1 L. B.	898	
Bundy, Marcus H.	1 L. B.	898	
Bundy, George L., Jr.	54	1035	(54) Mass. Wounded.
Bunker, Benjamin B.	1 H. A.	926	
Bunten, Alonzo	4	162	
Bunten, Alonzo	Band.	1035	
Buntin, Charles B.	1 H. A.	926	
Bunton, Sylvanus	2	36	
Bunton, Sylvanus	7	360	

MANCHESTER MEN IN THE CIVIL WAR—*Continued.*

NAMES.	Reg.	Page.	Remarks.
Bunton, Henry S.	7	360	
Burbank, Dennis V.	M. G.	995	
Burk, Leander	7	360	
Burke, Henry	7	360	
Burke, Henry	7	360	Deserted.
Burke, Patrick	8	413	Wounded.
Burke, William G.	4	162	
Burke, William G.	4	162	
Burr, Frank	1	5	
Burr, Frank	4	162	
Burrill, Warren A.	10	521	Wounded.
Burrill, Elisha H.	1 L. B.	898	
Burns, James G.	2	37	
Burns, James G.	1 H. A.	926	
Burns, James G.	N. G.	992	
Burns, James	4	162	Deserted.
Burns, James	10	521	Deserted.
Burns, John	8	414	
Burns, John	8	414	
Burns, Matthew	18	806	
Burns, Oliver	10	521	
Burns, Patrick	7	360	Died Sept. 14. '62.
Burns, Michael	2	37	Deserted.
Burns, Robert	1 L. B.	898	Deserted.
Burns, Thomas S.	4	162	
Burton, Henry	2	37	Wounded.
Burpee, Cyrus S.	8	414	
Burpee, Cyrus S.	V.R.C.	1005	
Bush, Orrin	4	162	Died July 16, '64.
Bustmew, James	8	414	Deserted.
Buswell, James M.	1 L. B.	898	
Butler, Daniel S.	10	521	
Butler, Eldad	10	521	Died Dec. 17. '63.
Byrns, Matthew	3	108	Wounded.
Cadorath, Eugene	3	108	Wounded.
Cadorath, Eugene	V.R.C.	1005	Died Nov. 14, '64.
Cahill, Francis	1	5	
Cahill, Francis	4	163	
Cain, Charles	7	361	Wounded.
Caldwell, John	8	414	Died Nov. 3, '62.

Names.	Reg.	Page.	Remarks.
Calef, Benjamin R.	N. G.	992	
Calef, George F.	N. G.	992	
Calef, William	2	37	Died March 29, '64.
Callender, Benjamin F.	1 V. C.	858	
Calley, John S.	2	37	Died April 15, '63.
Cameron, Abram	5	220	
Cameron, James	3	109	Wounded.
Campbell, John	2	38	
Campbell, John H.	8	414	
Campbell, Joseph	8	414	
Campbell, Alexander	10	521	
Campbell, Henry A.	1 L. B.	898	
Canara, Pasqual	Navy.	1106	Deserted.
Canfield, George	N. G.	992	
Canfield, Homer	1 L. B.	898	
Canfield, William A.	9	467	Wounded.
Cannon, Stilman P.	10	521	
Carey, Thomas F.	1	5	
Carey, Thomas F.	1 V. C.	834	
Carey, Henry F.	2	38	
Carey, Cornelius	10	522	Wounded.
Carey, Lawrence	11	1036	(11) Mass. Died Aug.
Carleton, Charles E.	9	468	[8, '64.
Carleton, George	10	522	
Carling, John	1 L. B.	898	Died Nov. 3, '65.
Carney, John	N. G.	992	
Carney, Michael	8	414	
Carney, William M.	3	109	Wounded.
Carpenter, James P.	1 L. B.	898	
Carr, James R.	2	38	
Carr, James R.	1 H. A.	927	
Carr, James R.	N. G.	993	
Carr, James W.	2	38	
Carr, James	1 L. B.	898	
Carr, Henry	12	612	
Carr, William	1 L. B.	898	
Carr, William	1 L. B.	898	
Carroll, Jeremiah	9	468	Wounded.
Carter, William H.	3	109	
Carter, William H.	3	109	Died Dec. 15, '64.

MANCHESTER MEN IN THE CIVIL WAR—*Continued.*

NAMES.	Reg.	Page.	Remarks.
Carter, Oscar E.	5	221	Died June 22, '62.
Casey, John	3	109	
Casey, John	8	415	Died Oct. 7, '62.
Casey, Thomas	3	109	
Cass, Albert	4	163	
Cass, Harrison S.	3	109	Wounded.
Casley, James	Navy.	1107	
Castallar, John M.	Navy.	1108	
Castello, Bryan	3	110	
Castello, Bryan	3	110	Deserted.
Castles, Patrick	4	163	
Caswell, Alonzo M.	1 L. B.	898	
Caswell, Augustus B.	1	5	
Caswell, John M.	10	522	Killed Sept. 30, '62.
Cate, Virgil H.	7	362	Killed July 18, '63.
Center, Benjamin L.	1 H. A.	908	
Center, James H.	1 H. A.	908	
Challis, Robert A.	3	110	
Chamberlin, Wm. N.	1 L. B.	898	Wounded.
Champlin, George H.	1	6	
Chandler, Benjamin	18	807	
Chandler, George M.	1	6	
Chandler, Jacob F.	8	415	
Chandler, James O.	1 H. A.	927	
Chandler, James O.	N. G.	993	
Chapman, Stephen C.	1	6	
Chapman, Stephen C.	4	163	
Chapman, Charles B.	10	522	Deserted.
Chapman, George W.	10	522	
Chapman, Jonathan B.	1 V. C.	834	
Chapman, Jonathan B.	1 V. C.	834	
Chase, John H.	1	6	Deserted.
Chase, John N.	3	110	
Chase, Benjamin F.	2	39	Killed July 2, '63.
Chase, Melvin	1	6	
Chase, Melvin	1 L. B.	898	
Chase, Moses L.	9	469	Deserted.
Chase, Stanford H.	1 H. A.	927	
Chase, Stanford H.	N. G.	993	
Chase, Hiram O.	10	522	Killed May 16, '64.

#### 43

MANCHESTER MEN IN THE CIVIL WAR—*Continued.*

Names.	Reg.	Page.	Remarks.
Chase, Charles J.	N. G.	993	
Chase, Israel W.	10	522	Deserted.
Cheney, Samuel	7	362	
Cheney, Royal	10	522	
Cheney, Thomas C.	1 L. B.	898	Wounded.
Chester, Wesley	18	807	Deserted.
Chickering, Charles	1 L. B.	898	
Chickering, Alpheus	3	110	Wounded. Deserted.
Childs, Jason N.	1 V. C.	834	
Childs, Jason N.	1 V. C.	834	Died Dec. 3, '64.
Choat, Elisha	19	1038	(19) Mass. Wounded.
Christenson, Andrew	2	39	
Chubb, John G.	1 V. C.	834	
Churchill, Herbert W.	1 H. A.	928	
Cilley, Anthony	7	362	Wounded. Dishonor-
Cilley, Ezra D.	1 L. B.	898	[ably discharged.
Cilley, Ezra D.	1 L. B.	898	
Cilley, Tristram	10	522	Wounded.
Clark, Benjamin F.	7	363	
Clark, Benjamin F.	7	363	Wounded.
Clark, Charles	1 L. B.	898	Deserted.
Clark, Charles A.	7	363	Killed July 18, '63.
Clark, George A.	7	363	
Clark, George A.	7	363	Died wds., May 11, '64.
Clark, George A.	10	523	Wounded.
Clark, George E.	1 V. C.	834	
Clark, Henry W.	1 L. B.	898	
Clark, Henry W.	1 L. B.	898	
Clark, John W.	1	6	
Clark, John F.	11	565	Died wds., Aug. 21, '63.
Clark, Joseph B.	11	565	Wounded.
Clark, Oliver H.	1 M. C.	1038	(1 M. C.) Mass.
Clark, Patrick	14	702	[Wounded.
Clark, Rufus F.	3	110	
Clark, Rufus W.	9	986	Killed Dec. 13, '62.
Clark, Warren	5	223	Deserted.
Clayton, Joseph	10	523	Deserted.
Clayton, Robert	4	164	
Clayton, Robert	4	164	Died Feb. 5, '65.
Clement, Abner H.	2	40	Deserted.

45

MANCHESTER MEN IN THE CIVIL WAR—*Continued.*

NAMES.	Reg.	Page.	Remarks.
Clifford. William A.	7	363	
Clifford, William A.	7	363	Wounded.
Clifton, Henry F.	2	40	
Clogston, Sylvester	8	416	
Clough, Albert N.	3	111	
Clough, Albert N.	1 V. C.	859	
Clough, Harrison M.	7	363	
Clough. Orrin A.	10	523	Died Wds., Aug. 17, '64.
Cobb, Willard K.	4	164	Killed Sept. 29, '64.
Coberey, John	8	416	Deserted.
Coburn, James H.	8	416	
Coburn, James H.	8	416	[dent.
Cochran, Jeremiah	4	164	Lost an arm by acci-
Cochran. John H.	10	523	Died Feb. 28, '63.
Cody, Walter	3	111	Wounded.
Cody. Walter	V.R.C.	1006	
Coffey. Jeremiah T.	3	111	
Cogswell, Edward P.	7	363	
Cogswell, Joseph H. L.	7	363	Died Jan. 4, '62.
Colburn, John C.	1 V. C.	860	
Colby, Abner D.	2 R. S.	977	
Colby. Abner D.	2 R. S.	977	
Colby. Abram P.	10	523	Wounded.
Colby. Isaac K.	4	165	
Colby. Isaac K.	4	165	Killed May 16, 64.
Colby. John F.	1 V. C.	834	
Colby, Matthew N.	1 V. C.	835	
Colby, Milo J.	18	808	
Colby, Daniel F.	3	111	Died Feb. 11, '62.
Colby, Harvey M.	2	41	Deserted.
Cole, John H.	2	41	
Cole, John H.	18	808	
Cole, Micajah S.	2	41	Deserted.
Cole, Micajah S.	6	1039	(6) Mass.
Cole, John S.	3	111	
Cole, John*	10	523	Killed Sept. 24, '62.
Cole, Charles H.	1 H. A.	928	
Coleman, John	2	41	Deserted.
Colley, Robert N.	8	416	Died May 18, '62.
Colligan, Michael.	2	41	Wounded. Deserted.

* Accidentally.

MANCHESTER MEN IN THE CIVIL WAR—*Continued.*

NAMES.	Reg.	Page.	Remarks.
Collins, James	7	364	
Collins, John	8	416	Died Oct. 14, '63.
Collins, Joseph	8	416	Deserted.
Collins, Thomas A.	1 V. C.	860	
Collins, Kitridge J.	1 L. B.	898	
Collins, James, Jr.	2 H. A.	915	
Collins, John L.	V.R.C.	1006	
Comfort, Alfred	1 H. A.	929	
Comfort, Joseph	1 H. A.	929	
Condict, Henry F.	1 L. B.	898	
Condict, Henry F.	8	1039	(8) Illinois.
Conet, George	1 H. A.	929	
Connell, Andrew M.	2	41	
Connell, John	8	417	Deserted.
Connelly, Patrick	3	111	Died May 22, '63.
Conner, George W.	10	523	
Conner, David A.	1 V. C.	860	Deserted.
Connolly, Michael J.	3	111	
Connolly, Michael	4	165	
Connolly, Michael	4	165	Died Sept. 12, '64.
Connolly, Morgan	10	524	
Connolly, Thomas	8	417	
Connolly, Thomas	U.S.A.	1040	
Connor, Charles O.	1	7	
Connor, Francis H.	1	7	
Connor, Francis H.	8	417	Wounded.
Connor, Francis H.	8	417	
Connor, Jeremiah	10	524	Wounded.
Connor, Jeremiah	V.R.C.	1006	
Conroy, James	1	1040	(1) Mass.
Conway, Patrick	4	165	
Conway, Patrick	4	165	Wounded.
Conway, Charles	8	417	Deserted.
Conway, Frederick	10	525	
Cook, Charles	8	417	Deserted.
Cook, Benjamin C.	18	808	
Coolidge, Lorin E.	1	7	
Cooper, James	12	614	
Cooper, Samuel	1 L. B.	898	Wounded.
Cooper, Alec	N. G.	993	

NAMES.	Reg.	Page.	Remarks.
Copp, John	7	364	Wounded.
Copp, John	18	808	
Copp, Harrison J.	3	112	Died April 27, '62.
Copps, Egbert M.	1	7	
Copps, Egbert M.	1 L. B.	898	
Corey, Augustus B.	18	808	
Corcoran, Michael	2	42	Wounded.
Corcoran, Michael	8	417	Wounded.
Corcoran, Michael F.	10	524	
Corcoran, Jeremiah	10	524	
Corliss, John S.	N. G.	993	
Corliss, Leonard B.	2	42	
Costello, John	2	42	Deserted.
Cotter, Edward	3	112	Wounded.
Coty, Gideon	3	112	Wounded.
Coty, Gideon	8	417	
Coughlin, John	10	524	Wounded.
Coughlin, Jeremiah	11	1040	(11) Mass.
Coughlin, Jeremiah	11	1040	(11) Mass. Wounded.
Cowan, Edward W.	18	808	
Cowley, Thomas R.	8	417	
Cox, Charles P.	1 L. B.	898	
Cox, Lemuel M.	2	42	
Coyle, George	2	42	
Craig, George W.	2	43	
Cram, George T.	1 V. C.	835	
Crawford, Joseph	8	418	
Cressy, Charles A.	1	7	
Cressy, Charles A.	4	166	Wounded.
Cressy, Amos	4	166	Died June 6, '65.
Cressy, Joseph P.	7	364	Died Dec., '64.
Cressey, Thomas E.	1 V. C.	835	
Crockett, Durrell S.	1 L. B.	898	
Crockett, John C.	1 H. A.	929	
Crooks, John	58	1040	(58) Mass. Wounded.
Crombie, James	10	524	
Corrigan, Owen	4	166	
Corrigan, Owen	4	166	
Croning, Frederick J.	1 L. B.	898	
Crosbie, Augustine	3	112	

MANCHESTER MEN IN THE CIVIL WAR—*Continued.*

NAMES.	Reg.	Page.	Remarks.
Crosbie, John	3	112	Killed July 10, '63.
Crosby, Alfred R.	1 L. B.	899	
Crosby, Alfred R.	1 L. B.	899	
Crosby, John L.	10	524	
Crosby. Patrick	8	418	Died Wds., June 15,'64.
Cross, Joseph	11	566	
Crowley, Cornelius	8	418	Died Wds., June 17,'63.
Crowley, John C.	10	525	
Crowley, John	8	418	Deserted.
Crowsan, John	3	112	Deserted.
Crumbie, Robert	7	365	Died April 9, '63.
Cuddy, Michael	4	166	
Cuddy, Michael	4	166	
Cuddy, Patrick	8	418	
Cuddy, Patrick	8	418	Wounded.
Cummings, James M.	4	166	
Cummings, James M.	V.R.C.	1006	
Cummings, Henry J.	3	112	
Cummings, Charles A.	9	471	
Cunningham, James	2	43	
Cunningham, Henry	6	1041	(6) Mass. Deserted.
Curchod, Eloi	12	615	Deserted.
Curley, James	2	43	
Curran, Daniel	8	418	Deserted.
Curran, John, 2d	3	113	
Curran, Patrick	10	525	
Currier, Andrew	V.R.C.	1006	
Currier, Hiram H.	10	525	
Currier, Charles M.	4	166	
Currier, Marcus M.	8	418	
Currier, Marcus M.	N. G.	993	
Curtis, Oren B.	V.R.C.	1006	
Cushing, Almus	4	166	
Cushing, John	2	43	Wounded.
Cushing, John	2	43	Deserted.
Cutter, William G.	1 L. B.	899	
Cutter, William G.	1 L. B.	899	
Daggs, William H.	C. T.	1018	
Daily, Thomas	1 V. C.	861	Deserted.
Daley, Dennis	28	1041	(28) Mass.

MANCHESTER MEN IN THE CIVIL WAR—*Continued.*

NAMES.	Reg.	Page.	Remarks.
Daley, James	8	418	Deserted.
Dakin, Edward W.	1 H. A.	930	
Dakin, Edward W.	N. G	993	
Dakin, George K.	1 L. B.	899	
Dakin, George K.	1 L. B.	899	
Dakin, George K.	U.S.A.	1041	
Dalton, Edward	4	166	Died Dec. 4, '61.
Dalton, Michael	10	525	Deserted.
Dalton, Thomas	12	615	Killed June 30, '64.
Damon, George B.	2	44	Deserted,
Darling, George	8	418	Deserted.
Darrah, Clinton A.	7	365	Died Oct. 24. '62.
Darrah, James W.	7	365	Died Feb. 14, '62.
Darrah, Silas L.	7	365	
Darrah, Silas L.	7	365	Deserted.
Dane, Albert G.	3	113	Wounded. Died Feb.
Davenport, Charles L.	7	365	[4, '65.
Davenport, Charles L.	6	300	
Davenport, Francis	8	418	Deserted.
Darivas, Alexander	14	704	
Davis, Charles	8	419	Deserted.
Davis, Charles F.	4	167	
Davis, Charles O. R.	3	113	Died June 30. '63.
Davis, Daniel	1 H. A.	930	
Davis, Daniel S.	7	365	
Davis, Daniel S.	10	525	
Davis, George W.	M. G.	995	
Davis, Hilas D.	5	227	Wounded.
Davis, James	18	809	Deserted.
Davis, James M.	2	44	
Davis, John F.	4	167	Deserted.
Davis, John B.	3	113	
Davis, John W.	10	525	
Davis, Joseph	7	366	Deserted.
Davis, Martin	12	616	Deserted.
Davis, Orrin D.	1 H. A.	931	
Davis, William	2	45	
Day, Alonzo L.	10	525	
Day, Alonzo L.	1 H. A.	931	
Day, John H.	1 H. A.	931	

NAMES.	Reg.	Page.	Remarks.
Day, Martin V. B.	1 L. B	899	
Day, Warren H.	1 H. A.	931	
Dearborn, Freder'k W.	2	45	Deserted.
DeMaranville, George	8	419	
Demarse, Joseph	10	525	
Demary, William E.	1 H. A.	931	
Demeritt, Charles H.	1	8	
Demeritt, Frank E.	1 L. B.	899	
Demeritt, Frank E.	V.R.C.	1007	
Demeritt, J. H.	Navy.	1115	
Dempcey, James C.	12	616	
Denyou, Michael	7	366	Wounded.
Derome, Edward	12	616	Deserted.
Desmond, Patrick	8	419	
Desmond, Patrick	V.R.C.	1007	
Devan, William	10	525	
Devine, Maurice	8	419	Died Dec. 22, '62.
Devine, Patrick	10	526	
Dewey, Jesse E.	2	45	
Dexter, George	2	45	Deserted.
Dickerman, William	11	568	Wounded.
Dickey, Chauncy C.	1 L. B.	899	Wounded.
Dickey, David B.	1 H. A.	931	
Dickey, Daniel H.	10	526	
Dickey, Henry C.	7	366	
Dickey, Henry C.	10	526	
Dickey, James M.	1 H. A.	931	
Dickey, James M., Jr.	4	167	
Dickey, James M., Jr.	4	167	Wounded.
Dickey, John	8	419	
Dickey, John W.	1 L. B.	899	
Dickey, John W.	1 L. B.	899	
Dickey, Lyman A.	2	46	Wounded.
Dignam, Walter	4	167	
Dignam, William	4	167	
Dignam, William	4	167	
Dillingham, Erlon V.	7	366	
Dillon, Edward J.	4	167	
Dimick, Charles N.	M. G.	995	
Dinsmore, Charles M.	1 H. A.	931	

57

MANCHESTER MEN IN THE CIVIL WAR—*Continued.*

NAMES.	Reg.	Page.	Remarks.
Dockum, Charles F.	1 H. A.	931	
Dodd, William	30	1043	(30) Mass.
Dodd, William	30	1043	(30) Mass. Wounded.
Dodge, Edwards O.	1	8	
Dodge, Hazen G.	7	366	
Dodge, Levi W.	N. G.	993	
Dodge, Reuben	1 H. A.	931	
Doe, Andrew W.	10	526	Killed Aug. 22, '64.
Doe, Charles A.	1 L. B.	899	Killed Dec. 13, '62.
Doherty, John	10	526	
Doherty, Peter	7	367	Died July 1, '64.
Doherty, Thomas	8	420	Died April 9, '63.
Doidy, Jeremiah	10	526	Deserted.
Dolton, James	2	46	Deserted.
Donnelly, John	2	46	Deserted.
Donnelly, Charles	2	46	Deserted.
Donnolly, Patrick	4	168	Deserted.
Donohoe, Joseph J.	3	115	Wounded.
Donohoe, Joseph J.	10	526	Wounded.
Donohoe, Cornelius	10	526	
Donohoe, Michael T.	3	115	
Donohoe, Michael T.	10	526	Wounded.
Donavan, Michael	10	526	
Donovan, James	4	168	
Donovan, Patrick	11	1043	(11) Mass. Deserted.
Doran, Michael	10	526	Deserted.
Doran, William	10	526	
Dorsey, Charles	C. T.	1018	Deserted.
Dougherty, James	7	367	
Dougherty, James	7	367	
Dougherty, Peter	8	420	Killed Oct. 27, '62.
Dow, Robert C.	3	115	
Dow, Jerome C.	V.R.C.	1007	
Dowd, John	8	420	
Dowd, Patrick	4	168	
Dowd, Patrick	4	168	Wounded.
Dowd, Patrick	8	420	Wounded.
Dowd, Patrick	V.R.C.	1007	
Dowd, Peter	Navy.	1116	Deserted.
Downes, Frank F.	7	367	

MANCHESTER MEN IN THE CIVIL WAR—*Continued.*

NAMES.	Reg.	Page.	Remarks.
Doyle, Edward	8	420	
Doyle, Patrick	10	527	Wounded.
Doyle, Daniel	1 V. C.	863	Deserted.
Dreggs, John	10	527	Died Oct. 9, '65.
Drew, Charles W.	10	527	
Drew, James M.	10	527	Deserted.
Driscoll, Jeremiah	8	420	
Driscoll, Patrick	8	420	
Driscoll, Patrick	18	810	
Drown, John	1 L. B.	899	
Drown, John	V.R.C.	1007	
Dudley, Hollis O.	1	8	
Dudley, Hollis O.	11	569	Wounded.
Dudley, George E.	11	569	Disabled, broke his leg.
Duff, James	10	527	Deserted.
Duffy, John, 2d	18	810	
Dugan, Peter	Navy.	1117	
Duggin, Edmund	10	527	
Dunbar, Charles D.	1	8	
Dunbar, George H.	1	8	
Dunbar, George H.	8	420	
Dunbar, George H.	8	420	
Dunbar, William E.	N. G.	993	
Dunham, George	8	420	
Dunham, Charles R.	1 V. C.	836	
Dunham, Emerson A.	1 V. C.	836	
Dunham, Emerson A.	1 V. C.	864	
Dunn, William	3	116	
Dunn, Andrew	10	527	Deserted.
Dupray, Joseph	3	116	
Dupray, Joseph	3	116	Deserted.
Duprey, Edward	1	8	
Dupree, Emile	2	47	Deserted.
Durant, John G.	1 H. A.	932	
Durbin, Francis	10	527	
Durgin, Joseph T.	1 L. B.	899	
Dustin, Eliphalet	4	169	
Duston, Jackson	1	8	
Duston, Jackson	4	169	
Duston, Jackson	4	169	

61

MANCHESTER MEN IN THE CIVIL WAR—*Continued.*

NAMES.	Reg.	Page.	Remarks.
Dwinells, Charles H.	7	368	Killed June 16, '64.
Earls, David	3	116	Wounded. Deserted.
Early, Michael	10	527	Wounded.
Earley, Patrick	10	527	
Eastman, Henry B.	1	8	
Eastman, Henry B.	3	116	Wounded.
Eastman, Henry B.	V.R.C.	1008	
Eastman, Frank A.	2	47	Killed July 21, '61.
Eastman, Moses L.	2	48	
Eastman, Freneto T.	9	475	
Eastman, Robert H.	19	1045	(19) Mass.
Eastman, William W.	V.R.C.	1008	
Eaton, Henry	M. G.	995	[27, '62.
Eaton, Eugene M.	22	1045	(22) Mass. Killed June
Edgerly, Andrew J.	4	169	
Edmands, Warren H.	9	475	Wounded.
Edmunds, Moses W.	1	8	
Edmunds, Frank L.	N. G.	993	
Edmunds, Frank L.	1 H. A.	933	
Edwards, James	8	421	Deserted.
Edwards, Henry	9	475	Deserted.
Egan, John	3	116	Wounded.
Egan, Owen	17	1045	(17) Mass. Wounded.
Eich, Englebert	5	231	Deserted.
Elliott, Charles	2	48	Died Wds., June 24,'64.
Elliott, Charles F.	1 V. C.	864	
Elliott, George H.	7	368	
Elliott, Thomas F.	3	117	Wounded.
Ely, Joseph	3	117	Died July 18, '64.
Emerson, Edward C.	11	569	Wounded.
Emerson, Orrin F.	10	528	Deserted.
Emerson, Thurlow A	2	48	Deserted.
Emery, Charles O.	3	117	
Emery, Charles O.	3	117	Killed May 13, '64.
Emery, Daniel	4	169	
Emery, Daniel	V.R.C.	1008	
Emery, Samuel E.	8	421	
Emery, Ira P.	10	528	
Esmire, Henry	10	528	
Esty, Charles J.	10	528	

MANCHESTER MEN IN THE CIVIL WAR—*Continued.*

NAMES.	Reg.	Page.	Remarks.
Evans, John M.	1	9	
Evans, John M.	3	117	
Evans, John M.	3	117	
Evans, John	5	232	Deserted.
Evans, Owen	18	811	
Everett, Henry H.	2	48	
Fargo, George W.	4	170	Wounded.
Farley, Bernard J.	2	49	
Farley, Daniel	3	117	Killed June 16, '64.
Farmer, Lucious	2	49	Deserted.
Farnham, James A.	4	170	
Farnham, Enoch T.	11	570	Died Wds., Dec. 13, '62.
Farnum, Calvin L.	7	369	Wounded.
Farnum, Calvin L.	V.R.C.	1008	
Farnum, George W.	M.G.	995	
Farrar, Howard M.	1 L.B.	899	Wounded.
Farrell, John	1 V.C.	865	
Farrey, Barnard	3	118	Wounded.
Farnsworth, Simeon D.	U.S.V.	1046	
Farrington, Michael	8	422	
Farrington, Michael	V.R.C.	1008	
Farrow, Sidney A.	2	49	
Favor, Frank W.	N.G.	993	
Fealty, Patrick H.	4	170	
Fearing, Hawkes, Jr.	8	422	
Fenton, Dennis	10	528	
Fergerson, William	18	812	
Ferguson, John	10	528	
Fern, James	4	170	
Ferrin, Frank	3	118	Deserted.
Ferry, James	4	170	
Ferson, Charles O.	3	118	
Ferson, Charles O.	3	118	Wounded.
Field, Edward	4	170	
Field, Edward	4	170	Wounded.
Field, Edward	C.T.	1019	Killed Feb. 11, '65.
Fife, John W.	1 L.B.	899	
Finn, Michael P.	10	528	
Finnean, Michael	8	422	
Fisette, Louis	2	49	

MANCHESTER MEN IN THE CIVIL WAR—*Continued.*

NAMES.	Reg.	Page.	Remarks.
Fish, Nelson C.	10	528	
Fish, John L.	1 L. B.	899	Died Wds., Dec. 14, '62.
Fish, William W.	11	570	Wounded.
Fisher, Heindrick	12	620	
Fisk, Wilbur	M. G.	995	
Fisk, Wilbur	1 H. A.	934	
Fisk, Ephraim	1 L. B.	899	
Fisk, Ephraim	1 L. B.	899	
Fitch, George E.	4	170	
Fitz, John	8	422	Deserted.
Fitzgerald, Maurice	8	422	
Fitzgerald, Thomas	8	422	
Fitzgerald, Thomas J.	8	422	
Fitzgerald, Thomas J.	8	422	
Fitzgerald, William	2	49	Wounded.
Flagg, Alpheus D.	4	170	
Flaherty, Thomas	8	422	Wounded.
Flanders, Harry J.	2	49	
Flanders, Alonzo M.	8	422	
Fleming, John	8	423	Died Aug. 20, '63.
Flemming, James	10	529	
Flemming, Thomas J.	4	171	
Fletcher, James F. W.	8	423	
Fletcher, James F. W.	8	423	
Flinn, Barney	18	811	
Flint, Frank A.	11	571	Wounded.
Flood, John	3	119	
Flores, Emanuel	8	423	Deserted.
Floyd, Andrew	12	620	
Flynn, Michael O.	1	9	
Flynn, Michael O.	4	171	
Flynn, James	8	423	Deserted.
Flynn, Thomas	8	423	
Flynn, William	2	50	Deserted.
Fogg, George I.	3	119	
Fogg, Benjamin F.	4	171	
Fogg, Benjamin F.	4	171	
Fogg, James M.	4	171	
Fogg, James M.	4	171	
Fogg, John	8	423	Deserted.

MANCHESTER MEN IN THE CIVIL WAR—*Continued.*

Names.	Reg.	Page.	Remarks.
Foley, David	3	119	Dishon. Disch'd.
Foley, Stephen	17	1047	(17) Mass. Deserted.
Foley, Stephen	3	119	Died Wds., Sept. 28, '63.
Foley, Laurence	8	423	
Foley, Maurice	4	171	
Foley, Maurice	4	171	Wounded.
Follen, Thomas	4	171	
Follon, John	4	171	
Follon, John	4	171	Wounded.
Fountain, Peter	3 C.	1048	(3 C) R. I. Deserted.
Forrest, George	12	620	
Forsaith, William R.	1 H. A.	935	
Fortier, Edmund	7	370	
Foss, Eugene K.	4	171	
Foss, Charles W.	10	529	Died Wds., June 11, '64.
Foss, Henry T.	1 H. A.	935	
Foss, Uriah H.	10	529	Wd. Died Nov. 6, '64.
Foster, William H.	3	119	
Fowler, Barnet E.	2	51	Deserted.
Fowler, John	8	423	Wounded.
Fowler, Patrick	10	529	
Fox, Michael	8	423	Deserted.
Fox, Thomas	8	423	
Fox, Patrick F.	10	529	Died July 20, '64.
Frank, William H.	2	50	
Frank, John	4	172	Deserted.
Fraser, Alexander	Navy.	1122	
Frawley, Terrence	4	172	
French, Austin G.	M. G.	996	
French, Charles L.	2	51	
French, Charles L.	2	51	
French, Charles F.	3	119	
French, Charles E.	1 L. B.	899	
French, Charles E.	1 L. B.	899	
French, James H.	1 V. C.	837	
Freschl, Joseph	7	371	
Frost, Hiram B.	4	172	
Frye, Andrew J.	11	572	Died Wds., May 16, '64.
Frye, Joseph P.	M. G.	996	
Fuller, Granville L.	7	371	

MANCHESTER MEN IN THE CIVIL WAR—*Continued.*

Names.	Reg.	Page.	Remarks.
Fuller, Granville L.	7	371	
Furnald, James G.	3	120	Wounded.
Furnald, James G.	3	120	Wounded.
Furnald, True O.	11	572	Wounded.
Gafney, Peter	8	423	
Gage, James D.	1 V. C.	837	
Gage, James D.	1 V. C.	837	
Gage, Horace P.	M. G.	996	
Gale, Israel N.	4	172	
Gallagher, Richard	10	529	Deserted.
Gallagher, Bernard	8	424	
Gallagher, John	8	424	Died April 22, '63.
Gallison, James P.	1 H. A.	935	
Galvin, Michael E. A.	3	120	
Galvin, Thomas J.	4	172	
Galvin, Thomas J.	4	172	
Gamble, John S.	1 H. A.	935	
Gannon, Thomas	8	424	
Gannon, William J.	8	424	Wounded.
Gauther, Joseph	18	812	Deserted.
Gardiner, James	9	478	
Gardner, John	1	9	
Gardner, John	4	172	Wounded.
Gardner, John	4	172	Killed Jan. 16, '65.
Gardner, Orrin S.	2	51	Deserted.
Gardner, Levi	3	120	
Gardner, Levi	3	120	
Gardner, Charles J.	6	307	Wounded.
Gardner, Charles H.	10	530	Wounded.
Gardner, Charles N.	M. G.	996	
Garland, Frank A.	4	172	Died June 4, '62.
Garland, Isaac	7	371	Wd. Died Nov. 2, '64
Garman, Elbridge G.	10	530	
Garnett, John	18	812	
Gartley, John	2	51	Deserted.
Gartna, Frederick	8	424	Deserted.
Garney, John	10	530	Wounded.
Gay, Thomas F.	3	120	
Gay, Paul	8	424	
Gemmell, William	4	173	Wounded.

MANCHESTER MEN IN THE CIVIL WAR—*Continued.*

Names.	Reg.	Page.	Remarks.
George, Albert	3	120	
George, Albert	3	120	
George, Charles	N. G.	993	
George, John	7	371	Deserted.
George, Samuel	1	10	
George, Samuel	3	120	
George, Samuel	3	120	Wounded.
German, James H.	4	173	Died June 1, '64.
Gerry, George	4	173	
Gerry, Elbridge	4	173	
Gerry, Elbridge	1 H. A.	936	
Gerry, John E.	4	173	
Gerry, John E.	4	173	Killed Jan. 16, '65.
Gerry, Madison	1 H. A.	936	
Gerry, Madison	N. G.	993	
Gibbons, John	8	424	
Gibson, John	2	51	
Gibson, Charles O.	3	121	
Gilbert, Charles	3	121	
Gilbert, Charles P.	M. G.	996	
Gilbert, Francis	8	424	
Gilbert, George	2	51	
Gile, Daniel	1	10	
Gile, Daniel	4	173	
Giles, Job R.	4	173	
Gill, Nicholas	7	371	Died July 31, '64.
Gillis, Louis J.	4	173	
Gillis, Louis J.	V. R. C.	1009	Deserted.
Gilman, George M.	8	424	
Gilman, George M.	8	424	
Gilman, Frank L.	1 H. A.	936	
Gilman, Frank L.	M. G.	996	
Gillmore, Thomas	7	371	Killed Feb. 20, '64.
Gilmore, Daniel S.	10	530	
Gilmore, William A.	1 H. A.	936	
Gladden, Jerry E.	1 L. B.	899	Deserted.
Glavin, James	3	121	Wounded.
Gleason, Joseph H.	2	52	
Gleason, Charles P.	4	173	
Gleason, Charles P.	4	173	

MANCHESTER MEN IN THE CIVIL WAR—*Continued.*

Names.	Reg.	Page.	Remarks.
Gleason, Patrick	8	425	Died Dec. 10, '62.
Glidden, John H.	1	10	
Glidden, Wesley	7	371	
Glines, Ezra B.	11	573	Wounded.
Glines, Humphrey M.	11	573	
Glines, George E.	1 L. B.	899	Wounded.
Glover, Noah	7	372	
Glover, David M.	10	530	
Goff, John	1	10	
Goggin, John	4	173	
Goodhue, Albert F.	1 H. A.	936	
Goodhue, Albert F.	M. G.	996	
Goodhue, Henry T.	N. G.	993	
Gogon, Thomas	10	530	
Goodwin, Charles F.	M. G.	996	
Goodwin, John W.	3	121	Died Wds., July 2, '62.
Goodwin, John H.	1 L. B.	899	
Goodwin, William H.	1 L. B.	900	Died Dec. 14, '62.
Gora, John	8	425	Deserted.
Gordon, Clark S.	1 L. B.	900	
Gordon, Clark S.	1 L. B.	900	
Gordon, George A.	1 H. A.	936	
Gordon, George A.	N. G.	993	
Gordon, Henry W.	1 H. A.	936	
Gordon, James H.	12	622	Wounded.
Gordon, Samuel	2 R. C.	1050	Deserted.
Gorman, Cyrus	3	121	Wounded.
Gorman, Charles H.	8	425	Deserted.
Gorman, James	4	173	
Gould, Page	1	10	
Gould, Stephen O.	4	174	
Gould, Stephen O.	V.R.C.	1009	
Gould, Luzern B.	9	479	
Gould, James P.	10	530	Died Wds., Oct. 27, '64.
Gould, Daniel W.	N. G.	993	
Gove, Eben	1 L. B.	900	
Gove, Hiram G.	V.R.C.	1009	
Gowing, Adams	7	372	
Gracey, William	3	122	
Gracey, William	3	122	

MANCHESTER MEN IN THE CIVIL WAR—*Continued.*

NAMES.	Reg.	Page.	Remarks.
Gracey, David	3	121	
Grammo, John	1 H. A.	936	
Grau, Jacob	1	10	
Graves, George W.	10	531	Died June 3, '64.
Gray, Charles R.	2	1051	(2) Mass.
Greager, Herman	4	174	
Greager, Herman	4	174	
Green, Charles E.	1 H. A.	937	
Green, Charles E.	M. G.	996	
Green, Charles P.	1 H. A.	937	
Green, Charles P.	N. G.	993	
Green, Frank S.	7	372	Deserted.
Green, Walter A.	3	122	
Green, Walter A.	18	813	
Green, Warren	1 H. A.	937	
Greenwood, Frank	7	372	Wounded.
Grey, Washington D.	1 L. B.	900	
Griggs, Julius H.	3	122	
Griffin, George W.	1	10	
Griffin, James	2	53	
Griffin, James F.	4	174	
Griffin, John	8	426	
Griffin, John	10	531	Wounded.
Griffin, Heber C.	7	373	
Griffin, Heber C.	1 H. A.	937	
Griffin, Heber C.	N. G.	993	
Griffin, Lyman W.	11	574	
Griffin, William H.	2	53	
Griffin, William H.	1 V. C.	868	
Griswold, George W.	1 L. B.	900	
Gross, David N.	11	1052	(11) Mass.
Grube, William	8	426	Deserted.
Guild, Royal E.	7	373	
Gunnison, E. Norman	2	54	
Gunston, William	4	174	Killed May 16, '64.
Gurry, Patrick	10	531	Killed Oct. 27, 64.
Guyon, Joseph	1	10	
Guyon, Joseph	2	54	Deserted.
Hackett, Frank B.	1	10	
Hackett, Frank B.	9	987	Wounded.

MANCHESTER MEN IN THE CIVIL WAR—*Continued.*

Names.	Reg.	Page.	Remarks.
Hackett, Edmond	3	122	
Hackett, Charles A.	4	174	
Hackett, George W.	4	174	
Hackett, George W.	4	174	
Hackett, John	4	174	Wounded.
Hackett, Thomas	2	1052	(2) Mass.
Hadlock, Charles H.	1 H. A.	936	
Hadlock, Charles H.	M. G.	996	
Haff, Martin A.	M. G.	996	
Hagerty, Daniel	8	426	Died Oct. 23, '62.
Haley, Daniel D.	10	531	
Haley, James	10	531	
Hall, Charles	1	11	
Hall, Charles	3	122	Died Apr. 11, '63.
Hall, Charles A.	1 H. A.	938	
Hall, Charles A.	M. G.	996	Died Feb. 12, '65.
Hall, Charles H.	10	531	Died Jan. 9, '63.
Hall, George H.	10	531	Wounded.
Hall, James T.	4	175	
Hall, John D.	1 L. B.	900	
Hall, John D.	1 L. B.	900	
Hall, Ezekiel	1 H. A.	938	
Hall, Leander E.	M. G.	938	Deserted.
Hall, Leander E.	1 H. A.	996	
Hall, Rufus	7	373	
Hall, Rufus B.	10	531	Died Dec. 11, '62.
Hall, William	7	373	
Halladay, Frank	3	123	Died Oct. 1, '62.
Hallissey, Timothy	Navy.	1127	Deserted.
Hamilton, Francis	7	373	
Hammer, Joseph	8	426	
Hammett, William E.	3	123	
Hammett, William E.	3	123	
Hamlett, Albert T.	1 L. B.	900	
Hamlett, Albert T.	1 L. B.	900	Wounded.
Hannaford, Abial A.	2	55	
Hannaford, Abial A.	2	55	
Hanberry, Michael	10	532	Wounded.
Hanchett, George	1 V. C.	837	
Hanson, George R.	2	55	Deserted.

MANCHESTER MEN IN THE CIVIL WAR—*Continued.*

Names.	Reg.	Page.	Remarks.
Hanson, Thomas	3	123	
Hanson, Elijah	2 R. S.	979	
Hanson, Rhodes	N. G.	993	
Haradon, Willard N.	9	481	
Haradon, Charles N.	1 V. C.	868	Died Oct. 19, '64.
Hardy, Charles T.	2	55	
Hardy, John C.	N. G.	993	
Hardy, William E.	3	123	Wounded.
Hardy, William E.	3	1053	(3) Vt. Wounded.
Harkins, John	7	374	
Harriman, Alfred J.	8	426	
Harriman, Benjamin F.	10	532	Wounded.
Harriman, Sylvester	8	427	Died June 25, '62.
Harrington, John	4	175	
Harrington, John	4	175	
Harrington, John	8	427	Wounded.
Harrington, Patrick	8	427	Deserted.
Harrington, Timothy	10	532	Deserted.
Harris, Charles E.	3	123	Wounded.
Harris, Charles E.	3	123	Died Nov. 30, '64.
Harris, George H.	4	175	
Harris, Hinckley D.	7	374	Wounded.
Harris, Joseph H.	10	532	Wd. Died Nov. 26, '64.
Harris, Michael	1 H. A.	939	Deserted.
Harrison, Thomas	8	427	Deserted.
Hart, William B.	4	176	
Hart, William H.	1 V. C.	837	
Hart, William H.	1 V. C.	837	
Hartley, Curtis R.	4	176	
Hartley, Henry	10	532	
Hartnett, John	8	427	Died Dec. 16, '62.
Hartshorn, Benj. L.	4	176	
Hartshorn, Jonathan	8	427	Died Sept. 18, '62.
Hartshorn, Joseph E.	9	481	
Hartshorn, Lowell S.	1 H. A.	939	
Harvey, Charles	3	123	
Harvey, Enoch T.	3	123	
Harwood, John	8	427	
Harwood, George	1 H. A.	939	
Haskell, William	4	176	

MANCHESTER MEN IN THE CIVIL WAR—*Continued.*

NAMES.	Reg.	Page.	Remarks.
Hastings, Cornelius	2	56	Wounded.
Hastings, George T.	10	532	
Hastings, Greeley W.	1 L. B.	900	
Hastings, Joshua K.	1 H. A.	939	
Hastings, William	10	532	
Hatch, Henry T.	3	124	
Hatch, John	7	374	
Hatch, John	7	374	
Hausman, John	3	124	Died Jan. 6, '62.
Hausman, Edward A.	N. G.	998	
Hayes, Henry	10	532	
Hayes, James	Navy.	1129	
Haynes, Martin A.	2	56	
Hazewell, Eugene G.	2	56	Wd. Died Apr. 2, '63.
Hazewell, Arthur W.	9	481	Killed May 12, '64.
Head, James	8	427	Deserted.
Healey, Timothy	3	124	
Healey, Timothy	3	124	Died wds., Dec. 12, '64.
Healey, Michael	8	427	Wounded.
Healy, Cornelius, Jr.	8	427	
Healy, Daniel F.	6	312	
Heath, Thorndike P.	2	56	
Heath, Thorndike P.	11	575	
Heath, Horace G.	4	176	
Heath, Horace G.	4	176	
Heath, Charles H.	12	624	Wounded.
Heath, Charles B.	7	375	
Heath, Thomas K.	7	375	Died Feb. 17, '62.
Heath, William O.	10	533	Died wds., Oct. 26, '64.
Hellfreich, Redolph	8	428	Dishon. discharged.
Hemmingway, Dan'l C.	7	375	
Hemmingway, Dan'l C.	7	375	
Henderson, James	3	124	
Henly, Michael	10	533	
Henly, Michael R.	16	1054	(16) Mass.
Henno, Israel	11	575	Wounded. Deserted.
Henry, William	10	533	
Hennessey, Maurice	3	124	Killed Aug. 16, '64.
Hennessey, John	7	375	
Hennessey, John	7	375	

MANCHESTER MEN IN THE CIVIL WAR—*Continued*.

NAMES.	Reg.	Page.	Remarks.
Hennessey, John	17	1054	(17) Mass.
Hennessey, James	8	428	Wounded.
Herlihy, Timothy C.	10	533	Deserted.
Hern, Lawrence	4	176	
Hern, Lawrence	4	176	
Heselton, Joseph	1	11	
Heselton, Joseph K.	15	747	Wounded.
Heselton, Joseph K.	10	533	Died Jan. 29, '65.
Heselton, Stilman B.	10	533	
Heselton, William W.	1	11	
Heselton, William W.	10	533	Killed Sept. 29, '64.
Hickman, William	5	240	Deserted.
Higgins, James	3	124	
Higgins, James	8	428	Deserted.
Higgins, William	10	533	
Hill, Harvey	2	57	Wounded.
Hill, Harvey	V.R.C.	1009	
Hill, Henry	3	124	
Hill, Henry	U.S.V.	1055	
Hill, Varnum H.	3	125	
Hill, Varnum H.	U.S.V.	1055	
Hill, Edward O.	4	177	
Hill, Edward O.	4	177	
Hill, James	8	428	Deserted.
Hill, Clinton C.	10	533	
Hill, Simon B.	7	375	
Hill, Sylvester J.	9	482	
Hill, Andrew	1 V. C.	869	Deserted.
Hill, Sullivan D.	1 H. A.	939	
Hill, William H.	3	125	Wounded.
Hills, James A.	7	375	
Hills, James A.	7	375	
Hilton, Charles C.	N. G.	993	
Hobart, John	7	375	
Hobbs, Edwin H.	1 L. B.	900	
Hobin, John	7	375	
Hobin, John	7	375	Wd. Died Nov. 12, '64.
Hodgkins, Sumner A.	1	12	
Hodgman, Edmond B.	7	375	Wounded.
Hodgman, Edmond B.	7	375	Wounded.

MANCHESTER MEN IN THE CIVIL WAR.—*Continued.*

NAMES.	Reg.	Page.	Remarks.
Hodgman, Charles H.	10	533	
Hodgman, Charles H.	1 H. A.	940	
Hodgeman, William S.	3	125	
Hohler, Herman K.	12	625	Deserted.
Hoit, John B.	9	987	
Holland, Richard F.	3	125	
Holland, John	8	428	Deserted.
Holcomb, Horace	10	533	Wounded.
Hollis, Newton	1 H. A.	940	
Hollis, Newton	N. G.	993	
Holmes, Andrew J.	3	125	
Holmes, Willard M.	2	58	
Holmes, Benjamin W.	14	1055	(14) Mass.
Holt, Wesley E.	1 L. B.	900	
Holt, Wesley E.	1 H. A.	940	
Holton, William M.	1 R. C.	838	
Hopkins, Cleaves W.	1 L. B.	900	
Hopkins, Henry F.	3	125	
Hopkins, Henry F.	1 V. C.	870	
Hopkins, Nathan E.	12	625	Deserted.
Hopkins, Philander	1 L. B.	900	
Hopkins, Philander	1 L. B.	900	
Horigan, John	10	534	
Horne, Richard J.	8	428	Deserted.
Hornsby, Thomas	12	625	Wounded.
Houghton, George C.	1 H. A.	940	
Houghton, George C.	M. G.	996	
Houghton, Ruthven W.	3	125	Wounded.
Houlihan, Patrick	8	429	Wounded.
Houlihan, Patrick	V. R. C.	1010	
House, James M.	2	58	Wounded.
Howard, Alfred	1 H. A.	940	
Howard, Alfred	M. G.	996	
Howard, Frank	5	242	Deserted.
Howard, James	2	59	
Howard, John	4	177	
Howard, John	12	625	
How, Edwin G.	1 H. A.	940	
Howe, John	8	429	Killed April 8, '64.
Howe, Henry N.	9	483	

NAMES.	Reg.	Page.	Remarks.
Howe, George H.	18	815	
Hubbard, George H.	2	59	
Hubbard, George H.	U.S.V.	1056	
Hubbard, George H.	10	534	
Hubbard, Joseph A.	2	59	Killed July 2, '63.
Hubbard, Luther P.	2	59	
Hubbard, Henry P.	1 V. C.	838	
Hubbard, Henry P.	1 V. C.	838	
Hubbard, Cyrus H.	4	178	Died July 16, '62.
Hubbard, Oliver	3	126	
Hubbard, Stimpson L.	2 R. S.	979	
Hubbard, William E.	8	429	
Hudson, William	2	59	Wounded.
Hulme, William	10	534	
Hulme, William	1 H.A.	940	
Hume, Robert	4	178	
Hume, Robert	4	178	
Hunkins, Moses A.	2	59	
Hunkins, Moses A.	V.R.C.	376	
Hunt, Lyford	4	178	
Hunt, Lyford	4	178	
Hunt, George J.	1 H.A.	940	
Hunt, George J.	N. G.	993	
Hunter, James	3	126	
Hunton, Dexter L.	10	534	
Huntress, Wilbur H.	3	126	
Huntress, Wilbur H.	3	126	Wounded.
Hurd, Charles W.	1	12	
Hurd, Charles W.	4	178	
Hurd, Charles W.	Navy.	1132	
Hurd, Charles H.	Navy.	1132	Died Jan. 23, '65.
Husted, George	8	429	Deserted.
Hutchins, Marshall	1	12	
Hutchins, Marshall	4	178	
Hutchins, Marshall	10	534	Deserted.
Hutchins, Melvin F.	4	178	
Hutchins, James S.	10	534	
Hutchinson, Frank B.	4	178	Killed May 16, '64.
Hutchinson, John G.	4	178	
Hutchinson, John G.	4	178	Wounded.

MANCHESTER MEN IN THE CIVIL WAR—*Continued.*

Names.	Reg.	Page.	Remarks.
Hutchinson, Frank	10	534	
Hutchinson, Justin	10	534	
Hutchinson, Alexander	11	577	Killed June 28. '64.
Hutchinson, Asa T.	9	987	
Hyatt, Lewis A.	M. G.	996	
Hynes, Dennis	1	12	
Hynes, Dennis	4	178	
Hynes, Dennis	4	178	Wounded.
Hynes, John R.	3	126	
Hynes, John R.	U.S.V.	1057	
Ingham, Ambrose	1 L. B.	900	Deserted.
Ingraham, William H.	8	429	
Jackman, George B.	18	815	Died May 8. '65.
Jackson, Joseph	1 V. C.	870	Deserted.
Jackson, Oliver	2 R. S.	979	
Jackson, Oliver	2 R. S.	979	
Jacobs, Timothy	18	815	Deserted.
Jacobsen, Carster	2	60	
Jadson, George H.	C. T.	1021	Died Oct. 21. '64.
James, Lemuel H.	4	179	
James, William	2	60	Deserted.
Janohow, John	2	60	Deserted.
Jefts, Henry S.	9	485	
Jenison, Charles O.	1	12	
Jenison, Charles O.	4	179	
Jenkins, James K.	10	534	
Jenness, George B.	5	244	
Jenness, James B.	1 V. C.	838	
Jenness, Joseph	1 H. A.	941	
Jeno, Joseph	18	815	Wounded.
Jepson, Oliver F.	1 H. A.	941	
Jewell, Frank C.	M. G.	996	
Johnson, Alonzo	1	1058	(1) Mass.
Johnson, Charles	10	535	
Johnson, Charles F.	11	577	Died Wds..Sept. 15,'64.
Johnson, Eleazer A.	10	535	
Johnson, George C.	3	127	Wounded.
Johnson, George B.	4	179	
Johnson, James	2	60	Deserted.
Johnson, John	18	815	

MANCHESTER MEN IN THE CIVIL WAR—*Continued.*

NAMES.	Reg.	Page.	Remarks.
Johnson, John E.	1 H. A.	941	
Johnson, John E.	M. G.	996	
Johnson, John E.	U.S.V.	1058	
Johnson, John H.	C. T.	1021	Died July 20, '65.
Johnson, Jonathan S.	2 R. S	979	
Johnson, William	3	127	Deserted.
Johnson, Moses H.	7	377	
Johnson, William	10	535	Deserted.
Johnston, Thomas	3	127	
Johnston, Thomas	3	127	
Johnston, Alexander	2	1058	(2) Mass.
Johnston, James A.	1 L. B.	900	Deserted.
Jones, Daniel	8	430	
Jones, Edwin R.	10	535	
Jones, Calvin A.	7	377	
Jones, Clinton	M. G.	996	
Jones, John A.	1 V. C.	838	
Jones, Philip	1 V. C.	838	
Jones, Philip	1 V. C.	838	
Jones, Robert	8	430	
Jones, Thomas	2	61	Wounded.
Jones, Thomas	10	535	Wounded.
Jones, Samuel	8	430	Deserted.
Jones, William	8	430	Wounded.
Jordan, Freeman F. B.	3	1058	(3) Mass.
Jordan, James A.	7	378	
Judd, Thomas G.	V.R.C.	1010	
Judkins, Howard	8	430	Deserted.
Junkins, Manly W.	1 H. A.	942	
Junkins, Melville P.	1 H. A.	942	
Kaine, John	8	430	
Kane, Charles	1 V. C.	838	Died Aug. 2, '62.
Kane, Michael	Navy.	1186	Deserted.
Kane, Thomas	8	430	
Kane, Thomas	V.R.C.	1010	Dishon. discharged.
Kaiser, Albert	2	61	
Kaskie, Samuel	11	578	Deserted.
Kating, John	1 H. A.	942	
Kean, Patrick M.	8	431	Died Jan. 10, '63.
Kearin, John	3	128	Dishon. discharged.

MANCHESTER MEN IN THE CIVIL WAR—*Continued.*

NAMES.	Reg.	Page.	Remarks.
Kearin, John	10	535	Wounded.
Kearin, Patrick	8	431	
Kearin, Timothy	8	431	
Keefe, Dennis	4	180	
Keefe, Robert	8	431	Deserted.
Keefe, William J.	8	431	
Keefe, William J.	8	431	
Keith., Marshall	M. G.	996	
Keller. Emile	4	180	Deserted.
KellererPatrick	18	816	Deserted.
Kelliher, John	3	128	Deserted.
Kelliher, John	8	431	Killed Oct. 27, '62.
Kelliher, Jeremiah	4	180	
Kelliher, Jeremiah	4	180	Died Oct. 9, '64.
Kelley, Daniel	1 L. B.	900	
Kelley, Charles J.	4	180	
Kelley, Francis	8	431	Died July 19, '62.
Kelley, James	8	431	Deserted.
Kelley, John	2	62	Wounded. Deserted.
Kelley, John	10	535	
Kelley, Owen	6	316	Wounded. Died Nov.
Kelley, William	2	62	[15, '64.
Kelley, William A.	1 V. C.	872	
Kelly, John L.	1	13	
Kelly, John L.	4	180	
Kelly, John L.	U.S.V.	1059	
Kelly, Joseph	1 H. A.	942	
Kelly, Patrick	8	431	Killed May 17, '64.
Kelly, Thomas	10	536	
Kenaston, Edgar D.	2	62	Died Mar. 4, '62.
Kenaston, Edwin R.	2	62	Wounded.
Kendall, Frank L.	1	13	
Kendrick, Wesley M.	10	536	Wounded.
Kennedy, Cornelius	4	180	
Kenney, Thomas	2	62	Deserted.
Kenney, Michael	8	431	Wounded.
Kenny, William B.	1 L. B.	900	
Kennison, Francis M.	7	378	Wounded.
Kensington, James	10	536	Deserted.
Kenson, George E.	N. G.	993	

MANCHESTER MEN IN THE CIVIL WAR—*Continued.*

NAMES.	Reg.	Page.	Remarks.
Kenrick, Stephen	1	13	
Kenrick, Stephen ·	4	180	
Kerr, Joseph	11	578	
Kershaw, Charles H.	8	431	Died Wds., June 14, '63
Kesler, James W.	11	578	Wounded.
Kidder, Charles S.	1 V. C.	838	Wounded.
Kidder, Charles S.	1 V. C.	838	
Kidder, George M.	4	180	Died Mar. 31, '65.
Kidder, George W.	Navy.	1137	
Kidder, Hiram D.	8	431	Wounded.
Kidder, Hiram D.	8	431	
Kidder, Nathan P.	1 V. C.	838	
Kidder, Nathan P.	1 V. C.	838	Wounded.
Kidder, Selwin J.	1 V. C.	872	
Killen, Henry	12	628	
Killey, Walter S.	15	749	
Kimball, Caleb J.	11	578	
Kimball, Edward P.	M. G.	996	
Kimball, Foster	10	536	
Kimball, Horace G.	1 H. A.	943	
Kimball, Ormand D.	1 H. A.	943	
Kinerson, Francis W.	18	816	
Kinerson, Josiah S.	1 H. A.	909	
Kirby, Daniel	3	129	
Kirby, Daniel	8	432	Wounded.
Kirby, David	10	536	
Kirwin, John	3	129	Wounded.
Kittridge, George W.	1	13	
Knight, Asa P.	1 H. A.	943	
Knight. George W.	1 H. A.	943	
Knight, Thomas	5	247	Deserted.
Knowles, Thomas L.	18	816	
Knowland, Hubbard	12	629	
Knowlton, Benjamin F.	10	536	Deserted.
Knowlton, Joseph H.	4	181	
Knowlton, Joseph H.	U.S.A.	1060	
Knowlton, William C.	7	379	
Knowlton, William H.	3	129	Wounded.
Knowlton, William H.	V.R.C.	1010	Deserted.
Knox, Daniel W.	4	181	

MANCHESTER MEN IN THE CIVIL WAR—*Continued.*

NAMES.	Reg.	Page.	Remarks.
Knox, Daniel W.	4	181	Killed Aug. 16, '64.
Knox, John R.	8	432	
Knox, John R.	8	432	Wounded.
Knox, William H.	3	129	
Knox, William H.	V.R.C.	1010	
Korner, William	2	63	Deserted.
Krusa, Jacob	9	487	Died Wds., July 7,'64.
Kyle, James J.	2	1060	(2) Mass.
Ladd, Daniel P.	1 L. B.	900	
Ladd, Dudley P.	1 L. B.	900	
Ladd, Joseph J.	1	13	
Ladd, Joseph J.	8	432	
Ladd, William O.	N. G.	993	
Lafayette, Frank	7	379	Deserted.
Laine, Cornelius	8	432	Wounded.
Laine, Michael	8	432	Died Wds., May 30, '63.
Lamarche, Azrie	18	816	
LaMudge, Alexander	3	129	Killed Aug. 26, '63.
Landers, John	10	536	
Lane, Dennis	8	432	
Lane, Dennis	8	432	
Lane, James	8	432	Deserted.
Lane, James	12	629	Deserted.
Lane, John	2	63	
Lane, John	12	1060	(12) Mass.
Lane, Perkins C.	2	63	
Langlais, Peter	28	1061	(28) Mass.
Langley, John F.	3	129	Wounded.
Langley, Orlando H.	7	379	Wounded.
Langley, Samuel G.	2	64	
Langley, Samuel G.	5	247	
Langley, Thomas B.	5	247	
Langmaid, J. Israel	8	432	Killed May 27, '63.
Lannegan, Daniel	1 V. C.	873	Deserted.
Larkin, James	4	182	
Larkin, Lawrence F.	10	536	Wounded.
Larkin, Patrick	3	129	Wounded.
Larkin, Patrick	3	129	Deserted.
Larson, Peter	2	64	Deserted.
Lathe, Freeman L.	9	487	

MANCHESTER MEN IN THE CIVIL WAR—*Continued.*

NAMES.	Reg.	Page.	Remarks.
Lathe, Hiram S.	9	487	
Lathe, Hiram S.	V.R.C.	1010	Dishon. discharged.
Lathe, James W.	9	488	Wounded.
Laven, Patrick	10	536	Deserted.
Lawrence, George F.	2	64	Wounded.
Lawrence, George H.	3	129	Killed July 26, '63.
Lawrence, Richard A.	2	64	
Lawrence, Richard A.	1 V. C.	839	
Lawson, George	20	1061	(20) Mass. Wounded.
Lawson, George	28	1061	(28) Mass. Wounded.
Lawson, William	1	13	
Leafe, Joseph	8	433	Wounded.
Leafe, Luke	3	130	Killed July 18, '63.
Leaks, Solomon	C. T.	1021	
Lear, John L.	1	14	
Learned, James W.	1 L. B.	900	
Learned, James W.	1 L. B.	900	
Leary, Jeremiah	2	64	Wounded.
Leary, Jeremiah	2	64	
Leavey, Denis	4	182	
Leavey, Denis	6 A. C.	1061	
Leavitt, Thomas M.	8	433	
Leavitt, Thomas M.	8	433	Wounded.
Lee, Charles H.	4	182	
Lee, Charles H.	18	817	
Lee, George W.	3	130	
Lee, George W.	3	130	Killed Aug. 16, '64.
Lee, Michael	8	433	
Lee, Patrick	3	130	Wounded.
Lee, Peter H.	10	537	Deserted.
Lee, Walter	Navy.	1139	
Leet, Levi H.	1 R. S.	969	Killed June 27, '62.
LeGranger, Charles	11	580	Deserted.
Leighton, John B.	M. G.	996	
Lemons, Joseph	2	65	
Leonard, Edward B.	8	433	
Leonard, Charles H.	10	537	Died Wds., June 20,'64.
LePorte, Odilon	18	817	Deserted.
Lescure, Louis	2	65	Deserted to the enemy.
Lesherville, Joseph	18	817	Died June 14, '65.

MANCHESTER MEN IN THE CIVIL WAR—*Continued.*

NAMES.	Reg.	Page.	Remarks.
Lettimer, John	8	433	
Lewis, George B.	10	537	Wounded.
Lewis, Henry	4	182	
Lewis, James	18	817	
Lewis, Levi B.	11	580	
Levert, Albert	2	65	Deserted.
Libby, Alvan H.	3	130	Killed July 18, '63.
Lifford, Julius	12	630	
Lindsey, John A.	18	817	
Lintner, J. Henry	12	630	Died Wds., May 27, '64.
Little, Henry F. W.	7	380	
Little, Henry F. W.	7	380	
Little, Henry F. W.	C. T.	1022	
Little, James M. T.	22	1062	(22) Mass.
Little, Samuel H.	3	130	Killed May 13. '64.
Livingston, Charles C.	4	182	
Lloyd, Robert	17	1062	(17) Mass.
Lockhart, Thomas	2	66	Deserted.
Lockwood, Albert N.	3	131	Deserted.
Loftis, Daniel	10	537	
Loomis, Oscar E.	1 H. A.	944	
Looney, Patrick	8	434	Wd. Died April 21, '64.
Lord, James J.	2	66	
Lord, William H.	N. G.	993	
Lougee, Frederick W.	4	183	
Lovely, Edward	10	537	Wd. himself purposely.
Lovett, John	4	183	
Lovett, Enoch	1 V. C.	839	
Lowd, Sedley A.	1 H. A.	944	
Lowell, Henry G.	7	381	
Lowell, Henry G.	7	381	
Lowery, Patrick	18	817	
Loyd, Robert	2	14	
Luce, Daniel	3	131	
Lunt, Frederick	8	434	Deserted.
Lunt, Eugene	9	489	
Lyford, John C.	7	381	
Lyford, Jeremiah D.	11	581	Died Dec. 9, '64.
Lynch, John	4	183	
Lynch, John	4	183	Wounded.

103

MANCHESTER MEN IN THE CIVIL WAR—*Continued.*

Names.	Reg.	Page.	Remarks.
Lynch, James	Navy.	1141	
Lyons, Dennis F. G.	8	434	Wounded.
Lyons, Dennis F. G.	U.S.V.	1063	Deserted.
Mace, Charles J.	1	14	
Mace, Charles J.	8	434	
Mace, Charles J.	8	434	
Mace, Samuel B.	4	183	
Mace, Samuel B.	4	183	
Mack, James	3	1063	(3) Mass.
Mack, John L.	4	183	Wounded.
Mack, Patrick	18	818	
Madden, Francis	10	537	
Madden, James	10	537	Killed June 16, '64.
Madden, Michael	4	183	Wounded.
Magoon, Charles D.	1 L. B.	901	
Magoon, David	18	818	
Magraw, John	12	631	
Maguire, Michael T. H.	10	537	
Maguire, M. Thomas H.	18	818	
Muguire, Scott	18	818	Deserted.
Mahany, Daniel, Jr.	3	131	
Mahany, Daniel, Jr.	3	131	Killed Jan. 16, '65.
Mahew, Charles H.	10	537	Wounded.
Mahoney, Michael	8	434	Wounded.
Mahoney, Michael	10	537	
Mahoney, Patrick	3	131	Wounded.
Mahoney, Timothy	8	434	
Major, William	1	14	
Maloney, Bartholomew	4	183	
Maloney, Edward	25	1063	(25) Mass.
Maloney, James	1 H. A.	945	Deserted.
Malone, John	4	183	
Malone, John	4	183	Died May 18, '64.
Manning, Frederick S.	1	14	
Manning, Patrick	8	434	
Manning, Patrick	8	434	Wounded.
Manning, Rodney A.	2	67	Killed Aug. 1, '63.
Manter, George W.	3	131	
Mara, Michael	10	538	
Marble, Joseph R.	V.R.C.	1011	

MANCHESTER MEN IN THE CIVIL WAR—*Continued.*

Names.	Reg.	Page.	Remarks.
Marckres, Samuel D.	1	14	
Marckres, Samuel D.	4	184	
Marckres, Samuel D.	4	184	
Marden, Charles T.	4	184	
Marden, Charles T.	4	184	Wounded.
Marden, George W.	10	538	
Mardin, Michael	1	14	
Markham, John G.	7	381	
Markham, John G.	7	381	
Marsh, Charles C.	4	184	
Marsh, Charles C.	4	184	
Marsh, John B.	11	581	['65.
Marshall, Calvin C.	12	1064	(12) Me. Died May 6.
Marshall, Dustin	3	132	Wounded.
Marshall, Horace P.	1 L. B.	901	
Marshall, Nathaniel	3	132	Died Wds., July 15,'62.
Martin, Charles	14	1064	(14) Mass.
Martin, Charles H.	15	751	Wounded.
Martin, Charles H.	1 H. A.	945	
Martin, George A.	1 H. A.	945	
Martin, Hazen B.	2	67	
Martin, John	10	538	
Martin, John	10	538	Died Aug. 8, '64.
Martin, Joseph	11	582	Deserted.
Martin, Joseph	12	631	Wounded.
Martin, William H.	1	14	
Martins, George	8	435	Deserted.
Mason, Charles	2	67	
Mason, Daniel W.	7	382	
Mason, Granville P.	7	382	
Mason, John A.	2	67	
Mason, John A.	4	184	
Mason, John A.	10	538	
Mason, John E.	9	489	
Mason, William F.	9	489	Died Dec. 10, '62.
Masterson, William	18	818	
Matthews, Frank	4	184	
Maxwell, William H.	3	132	Wounded.
May, Daniel W.	4	184	
May, Edward	7	382	

MANCHESTER MEN IN THE CIVIL WAR—*Continued.*

NAMES.	Reg.	Page.	Remarks.
Mayers, James	3	132	Killed June. 16, '62.
Mayhew, George E.	1 H. A.	946	
Mayne, William W.	1	15	
Mayne, William W.	4	184	Wounded.
McAnally, Robert	1	15	
McCabe, George F.	7	382	
McCabe, Edward	8	435	
McCabe, Edward	8	435	Deserted.
McCabe, Thomas	7	382	
McCann, William	8	435	
McCartee, John	18	818	
McCarthy, Daniel	3	132	[to the enemy.
McCarthy, Daniel	20	1064	(20) Maine. Deserted
McCarthy, John	8	435	Killed April 15, '64.
McCarthy, Timothy	8	435	Died Wds., July 18,'63.
McCarty, Charles	10	538	Wd.Died March 22,'64.
McCarty, Daniel	8	435	
McCarty, Dennis, 1st	8	435	
McCarty, Dennis, 1st	8	435	Deserted.
McCarty, Dennis, 2d	8	435	
McCarty, Eugene	1	15	
McCarty, Eugene	7	382	Wounded.
McCarty, James	7	382	Killed Feb. 20, '64.
McCarty, Patrick	10	538	
McCarty, Patrick	12	631	
McCauley, John	1 H. A.	946	
McClemens, John	3	132	Wounded.
McConnell, John	12	631	Wounded.
McCormick, George	2	68	Deserted to the enemy.
McCormick, Jacob	12	631	Died Wds.,June 14,'64.
McCormick, James	8	435	Deserted.
McCullough, Patrick	8	435	
McDermott, Hugh	8	435	Died Sept. 30, '62.
McDole, Samuel	4	185	Wounded.
McDonald, James	8	435	
McDonald, John	2	68	
McDonald, Walter	7	382	
McDonald, Walter	7	382	Wounded.
McDonough, Patrick	4	185	
McDowell, Robert	9	987	Deserted.

MANCHESTER MEN IN THE CIVIL WAR—*Continued.*

NAMES.	Reg.	Page.	Remarks.
McEnery, Thomas	3	133	
McEwen, James	3	133	Wounded.
McFarland, David	7	383	Died Aug. 31, '64.
McFarland, Robert J.	18	818	
McFee, John	18	818	
McGarrett, William A.	9	490	Wounded.
McGinness, Arthur	2	68	Deserted.
McGlauflin, Charles A.	2	68	
McGlauflin, Charles A.	2	68	Wounded.
McGrath, Patrick	2	68	Deserted.
McGuiness, John	1	15	
McHugh, Michael	4	185	
McHugh, Michael	4	185	Deserted.
McInnis, Angus	10	539	
McIntire, Daniel	8	435	Died Oct. 3, '63.
McIntire, Hugh	8	435	
McIntire, John	3	133	
McIntire, John	3	133	Died Nov. 14, '64.
McIntire, William	8	435	Wounded.
McIntyre, George S.	8	435	Deserted.
McKinnon, George	12	1065	(12) Mass.
McKinnon, George W.	1	15	
McKinnon, George W.	2	69	Wounded.
McKinnon, Malcolm	1	15	
McKinnon, Malcolm	2	69	Wounded.
McKinnon, Malcolm	V.R.C.	1011	
McKinnon, Walter H.	2	69	
McLaughlin, Patrick	8	435	
McLee, Patrick	4	186	
McManus, Hugh	10	539	
McMellen, Daniel	8	436	Killed July 6, '63.
McNally, Daniel	8	436	Died Wds., June 14, '63
McNally, James	8	436	Wounded.
McNeil, Andrew	3	133	Deserted.
McPherson, William F.	10	539	
McQuestion, Jerome B.	3	133	
McQueston, Samuel F.	16	780	Died June 13, '63.
McQueston, Leroy	1 L. B.	901	
Meagher, James	8	436	Wounded.
Meagher, James	8	436	

MANCHESTER MEN IN THE CIVIL WAR—*Continued.*

NAMES.	Reg.	Page.	Remarks.
Melendy, Bryant H.	1 L. B.	901	
Mellen, Charles A.	11	583	Wounded.
Merrill, Bradley	1 H. A.	946	
Merrill, Darius	7	383	
Merrill, Frederick G.	7	383	
Merrill, Harry O.	10	539	
Merrill, John S.	7	383	Wounded.
Merrill, Joseph G.	9	491	Wounded.
Merron, James	4	186	
Merron, James	4	186	
Metcalf, Nathan H.	1 H. A.	946	
Mettimus, Edward	8	436	Died Wds., May 27, '63
Michau, Pierre	1 H. A.	946	Died March 26, 65.
Milan, John	8	436	
Milan, John	8	436	Deserted.
Milan, William	10	540	
Miles, James	8	436	
Miles, James	8	436	
Miller, Albert	Navy.	1147	
Miller, Carl	8	436	
Miller, John	2	70	
Miller, John	8	437	Deserted.
Miller, Joseph L.	4	186	
Miller, Peter	8	437	
Miller, Peter	8	437	Died Oct. 4, '64.
Mills, Charles	8	437	Deserted.
Mills, Hugh	1 V. C.	840	
Mills, Hugh	1 V. C.	840	Wounded.
Minhan, John	8	437	
Minhan, John	8	437	Deserted.
Mitchell, Edward I.	2	70	
Mitchell, Isaac	10	540	
Mitchell, John W.	7	384	Died Aug. 26, '65.
Mitchell, Lewis J.	9	491	Deserted.
Mitchell, Samuel L.	10	540	Wounded.
Mix, Daniel	2	70	Deserted.
Mokler, James	4	187	Wounded.
Monroe, James S.	8	437	
Monroe, James S.	8	437	
Mooar, Oscar A.	2	71	Died July 31, '63.

MANCHESTER MEN IN THE CIVIL WAR—*Continued.*

Names.	Reg.	Page.	Remarks.
Moore, David	3	134	
Moore, David	3	134	
*Moore, Frank	7	384	Captured by the enemy.
Moore, Frederick D.	4	187	Killed May 16, '64.
Moore, George C.	18	819	Died Feb. 23, '65.
Moore, Lewis D.	17	1066	(17) Mass.
Moore, Thomas T.	3	134	
Moore, William	8	437	Deserted.
Moore, William J.	1 H.A.	947	
Morgan, Charles	3	134	Died Wds.,Aug. 27,'62.
Moriarty, Bartholomew	8	437	
Moriarty, Cornelius	8	437	
Moriarty, Cornelius Jr.	8	437	Died Wds., May 3, '63.
Moriarty, Eugene	8	437	
Morrill, Frank L.	3	134	Died Wds., July 13,'64.
Morrill, Joseph A.	11	1067	(11) Mass. Died Wds.,
Morrill, Joseph B.	1 V.C.	840	Deserted. [Aug. 2, '63.
Morrill, Thomas W.	1 L.B.	901	Killed Dec. 13, '62.
Morrill, William W.	7	385	
Morrill, William H.	8	438	
Morrison, Charles H.	1	15	
Morrison, Charles L.	10	540	
Morrison, Albert B.	N.G.	993	
Morrison, Dan S.	3	134	
Morrison, John	14	1067	(14) Mass.
Morrison, Thaddeus K.	4	187	Discharged by sentence
Morrow, Matthew	M.G.	996	[G. C. M.
Morse, Charles E.	M.G.	996	
Morse, Elijah A.	2	71	
Morton, Henry	18	819	Deserted.
Moulton, Charles H.	M.G.	996	
Mudd, Thomas	C.T.	1022	
Mulaskey, James	4	187	Wounded.
Mullen, John	4	187	
Mullen, John	4	187	Wd. Died July 29, '64.
Mullen, John	8	438	
Mullen, Michael	8	438	
Mullen, Michael	V.R.C.	1011	
Mulligan, Edward	18	819	
Mulligan, Edward	17	1067	(17) Mass.

*Enlisted in the Confederate army.

NAMES.	Reg.	Page.	Remarks.
Mulligan, Michael	7	385	
Mulligan, Michael P.	18	819	Deserted.
Mulligan, Patrick	10	541	Died Wds.. July 11.'64.
Mulligan, Thomas	10	541	
Mullins, Michael	2	72	
Mumford, Albert	12	634	
Murdough, George	3	135	
Murphy, Dennis	8	438	
Murphy, Henry	4	188	
Murphy, Hugh	10	541	
Murphy, James	4	188	Deserted.
Murphy, John	4	188	
Murphy, John	8	438	Wounded.
Murphy, John	10	541	
Murphy, John	10	541	Deserted.
Murphy, John	10	541	Wounded.
Murphy, Thomas	8	438	Wounded.
Murphy, Thomas	8	438	Deserted.
Murphy, Thomas	10	541	Deserted.
Murray, Daniel	2	72	
Murray, Michael	8	439	
Murray, Robert P.	3	135	
Murray, William	V.R.C.	1011	
Murry, James	9	492	
Murry, Thomas	10	541	
Myears, John	5	256	Deserted to the enemy.
Myer, Charles	8	439	Deserted.
Myers, Charles	8	439	
Myers, Louis	9	493	
Nahan, Daniel	8	439	Died June 18. '65.
Neal, Aldano	N. G.	993	
Nelson, Albert F.	10	541	
Nelson, David B.	1 V. C.	840	
Nelson, George	2	73	Deserted.
Nelson, Sylvester W.	4	188	
Nevin, Patrick	10	541	
Newell, Daniel W.	2	73	
Newell, George W.	10	541	
Newell, Samuel	2	73	
Newell, Thompson L.	4	188	

MANCHESTER MEN IN THE CIVIL WAR—*Continued.*

NAMES.	Reg.	Page.	Remarks.
Newton, Charles A.	4	188	
Newton, Charles A.	4	188	
Newton, David H.	3	136	
Newton, Henry E.	1 V. C.	840	
Newton, Henry E.	1 H. A.	948	
Newton, John	2	73	Wounded. Deserted.
Nichols, George	5	257	
Nichols, George W.	1 H. A.	948	
Nichols, Herman	4	188	
Nichols, Jonathan P.	4	188	
Nichols, Jonathan P.	V.R.C.	1011	
Nichols, William G.	3	136	
Niles, Stephen W.	3	136	
Norris, Cyrus B.	9	987	
Norris, Henry C.	1 H. A.	948	
Norris, Henry C.	N. G.	993	
Norton, John F.	8	439	
Norrop, Lewis	14	719	
Nourse, Ozro N.	1 H. A.	948	
Noyes, Fairfield	2	73	Died Dec. 16, '61.
Noyes, Henry R.	1 L. B.	901	
Noyes, Hezekiah H.	1 H. A.	948	
Nutting, Eben H.	4	189	
Oakley, Henry	4	189	
O'Brian, John	4	189	
O'Brien, Daniel	10	541	
O'Brien, Dennis	8	439	Died Nov. 30, '62.
O'Brien, Edmond	3	136	
O'Brien, John	8	440	
O'Brien, John	8	440	
O'Brien, John L.	10	541	Wounded.
O'Brien, John P.	10	541	Wounded.
O'Brien, Michael	14	719	
O'Brien, Patrick	10	542	
O'Brien, Peter	1	16	
O'Brien, Peter	4	189	
O'Brien, Peter	4	189	
O'Brien, Terrence	3	136	Wounded.
O'Brien, Terrence	13	678	
O'Connell, Robert	3	136	Wounded.

MANCHESTER MEN IN THE CIVIL WAR—*Continued.*

NAMES.	Reg.	Page.	Remarks.
O'Conner, Patrick	4	189	
O'Connor, Charles	8	440	Wounded.
O'Connor, James	5	258	
O'Connor, Timothy	8	440	Killed June 14, '63.
O'Connor, William D.	8	440	
O'Day, Patrick	7	386	
O'Day, Patrick	7	386	
O'Donnell, William	8	440	
Offutt, Charles W.	1 L. B.	901	[G. C. M.
O'Flynn, John	10	542	Discharged by sentence
Ogden, John E.	2	74	
O'Grady, Edward	3	136	
O'Grady, Michael	8	440	Wounded.
O'Hara, John	1 V. C.	878	Deserted.
Oliver, Olden	18	820	Deserted.
Oliver, Samuel H.	2	74	
O'Melie, Joseph	10	542	Died Wds., June 25,'64.
O'Neil, James	3	136	
O'Neil, James	3	136	Died April 11, '64.
O'Neill, Felix	8	440	Wounded.
O'Neill, Michael	8	440	
Ormsby, Albert G.	4	189	
Ormsby, Albert G.	4	189	
Ordway, William F.	1	16	
Ordway, William F.	10	542	Died Dec. 17, '62.
Osborn, Henry	7	386	Wounded.
Osgood, Henry C.	4	189	
Osgood, Henry C.	4	189	Wounded.
Osgood, Ira S.	M. G.	996	
Osgood, Joseph C.	10	542	
O'Sullivan, Dennis	8	440	
Oswald, Martin	12	635	Wounded. Deserted.
Packard, Edwin R.	1 V. C.	878	
Page, Chester L.	1 H.A.	949	
Page, Frederick T.	4	189	
Page, Frederick T.	6 A. C.	1069	
Page, John G.	1 V. C.	840	
Page, John G.	1 V. C.	840	
Page, Theodore L.	8	440	Died Sept. 8, '62.
Paige, Frank W.	11	586	

MANCHESTER MEN IN THE CIVIL WAR—*Continued.*

NAMES.	Reg.	Page.	Remarks.
Paige, Harlan E.	4	189	
Paige, Henry C.	V.R.C.	1012	
Paige, Hiel B.	7	386	
Paine, Frederick	1 H. A.	949	
Paine, Patrick	10	542	
Palmer, George A.	1 H. A.	949	
Palmer, George A.	M. G.	996	
Palmer, Irving S.	1 L. B.	901	Wounded.
Palmer, Stephen H.	2	74	Died Wds., Aug.14,'63.
Palmer, William	8	440	Deserted.
Palmer, William H.	1 V. C.	840	
Palmer, William H.	1 V. C.	840	
Parker, Benjamin K.	1 H. A.	949	
Parker, Charles I.	D. C.	1094	
Parker, Christopher	1 H. A.	949	
Parker, Cornelius E.	4	189	
Parker, Charles M.	2	74	Wounded. Deserted.
Parker, Francis W.	4	189	Wounded.
Parker, George	7	387	
Parker, George	7	387	Died Nov. 22, '64.
Parker, George	12	635	
Parker, George A. W.*	11	586	Killed March 31, '64.
Parker, Henry C.	1 L. B.	901	Killed Aug. 29, '62.
Parker, Horace H.	4	189	
Parker, John	10	542	Deserted.
Parker, Timothy	3	137	
Parks, James H.	1 V. C.	878	
Parquet, Henry	1 H. A.	910	Wounded.
Parrett, Charles F.	2	75	Killed July 2. '63.
Parrett, George W.	1 L. B.	901	
Paul, Charles H.	7	387	
Paul, Charles H.	7	387	
Peacock, James	11	586	Wounded.
Peake, James	2	75	Wounded.
Pearson, Charles	1 L. B.	901	
Pearson, Moses O.	1 H. A.	949	
Pearson, William S.	1	16	
Pearson, William S.	1 H. A.	949	
Peavey, Daniel M.	1 L. B.	901	Deserted.
Peeples, Charles	1 L. B.	901	

* By a citizen of Stamford, Kentucky.

NAMES.	Reg.	Page.	Remarks.
Pelkey, Peter	3	137	
Pelkey, Peter	3	137	Wounded.
Pennock, Jonathan C.	M. G.	996	
Peno, Joseph	10	542	
Percival, William H.	10	542	Deserted.
Perkins, David M.	2	75	
Perkins, Charles G.	2	1070	(2) Mass. Deserted.
Perkins, Joseph	10	543	
Perkins, Oscar	4	190	
Perkins, Oscar	4	190	Wounded.
Perkins, William D.	1 L. B.	901	
Perkins, William H.	4	190	
Perry, Austin E.	3	138	
Perry, Austin E.	3	138	
Perry, Albert Q.	10	543	Wounded.
Perry, George F.	2	76	Wounded.
Perry, George F.	V.R.C.	1012	
Perry, George T.	7	387	
Perry, Jewett W.	1 V. C.	879	Died July 11, '65.
Perry, Stephen H.*	15	753	
Pervier, Amasa J.	3	138	Wounded.
Pervier, Amasa J.	4	190	
Pervier, Amasa J.	18	820	
Peters, Charles E.	1	1070	(1) Vermont.
Peters, John	2	76	
Pettengall, John F.	8	441	Died June 7, '63.
Pettingill, Lafayett	6	328	
Pickersgill, Henry J.	16	1071	(16) Mass.
Plumpton, Ephraim	1 V. C.	879	
Phelan, Richard	8	441	
Phelps, John L.	11	587	Died Nov. 10, '64.
Phelps, Levi	12	636	
Philbrook, Thomas P.	4	190	
Philbrick, Benjamin F.	8	441	
Philbrick, Benjamin F.	8	441	
Philbrick, Benjamin F.	1 V. C.	879	
Philbrick, Preston	7	387	Died Dec. 2, '62.
Phillips, Francis H.	1 V. C.	841	
Pickard, Horace C.	18	820	
Pickett, John	4	190	

*Henry S. Perry.

Names.	Reg.	Page.	Remarks.
Pickett, John	4	190	
Pickup, George	2	76	Wounded.
Pierce, Elihu P.	6	328	
Pierce, Nathan H.	8	441	
Pierce, Nelson J.	4	190	Killed June 5, '64.
Pierce, Samuel W.	1	17	
Pierce, Thomas P.	2	76	
Pierce, William L.	1	17	
Pike, Francis H.	1	17	
Pike, Francis H.	4	190	
Pike, Francis H.	10 A.C.	1002	
Pike, Timothy H.	2	76	
Pillsbury, Henry M.	2	76	
Pillsbury, Henry M.	1 H. A.	950	
Pillsbury, Orrin F.	1 H. A.	950	
Pinder, John	Navy.	1155	Deserted.
Pinkham, William W.	10	543	Died Feb. 26, '65.
Piper, John K.	1 L. B.	901	
Piper, Samuel S.	1 L. B.	901	Wounded.
Piper, William A.	1 V. C.	879	
Place, Zelotus L.	10	543	Wounded.
Platt, James H.	2	77	Killed May 16, '64.
Plummer, Thomas A.	8	441	Died July 20, '62.
Plummer, William H.	18	821	
Plunkett, Charles	10	543	Deserted.
Ponden, John	10	543	
Porter, Charles P.	Navy.	1156	
Porter, Charles P.	Navy.	1156	
Porter, Francis L.	1 V. C.	841	Wounded.
Porter, Samuel A.	4	191	
Porter, Solon F.	2	77	Died Mar. 14, '62.
Potter, Frank L.	4	191	Killed July 8, '64.
Potter, Joseph	3	138	Wounded.
Potter, Lewis	3	138	
Powell, Thomas	Navy.	1156	Deserted.
Powers, John H.	4	191	Wounded.
Powers, Joshua	10	543	Died Nov. 20, '62.
Powers, Michael	V.R.C.	1012	Deserted.
Powers, Richard	11	1071	(11) Mass.
Powers, William C.	1 V. C.	841	

MANCHESTER MEN IN THE CIVIL WAR—*Continued.*

NAMES.	Reg.	Page.	Remarks.
Powers, William C.	1 V. C.	841	
Prescott, Charles L.	1 V. C.	841	
Prescott, Charles L.	1 V. C.	841	
Prescott, Delano	10	543	
Prescott, James T.	9	496	
Prescott, John H.	M. G.	996	
Preston, John	23	1072	(23) Illinois.
Proctor, Orlando	1 H. A.	951	
Proudman, James D.	3	139	
Provencher, Joseph E.	9	987	Wounded.
Putnam, Byron	4	191	
Putnam, Charles	N. G.	994	
Putnam, George W.	7	388	
Putnam, George W.	7	388	Deserted.
Putnam, Levi	4	191	
Putney, Charles A.	8	422	
Pyer, Charles G.	7	388	
Pyer, Charles G.	7	388	Wounded.
Quigley, James	8	442	Deserted.
Quimby, Benjamin K.	4	192	
Quimby, David A.	10	543	Died Mar. 11, '64.
Quimby, Geo. W., Jr.	26	1072	(26) Mass.
Quimby, Henry L.	10	543	Deserted.
Quimby, James M.	2	77	
Quimby, James M.	1 H. A.	951	
Quimby, Jonathan C.	2	78	
Quimby, Albert F.	1 H. A.	951	
Quimby, Moody	1 V. C.	841	
Quimby, Moody	1 V. C.	841	
Quimby, Moses E.	10	543	Wounded.
Quimby, Thomas B.	10	544	Died Jan. 28, '65.
Quinby, Elisha T.	8	442	
Quinby, Elisha T.	V.R.C.	1012	
Qaindley, Benjamin F.	8	442	Died Jan. 1, '64.
Quinlan, James	3	139	
Quinlan, James	3	139	Wounded.
Quinlan, Jeremy	3	139	
Quin, Andrew	2	78	Deserted.
Quinn, Edward	3	139	Killed June 16, '62.
Quinn, Frank	4	192	

MANCHESTER MEN IN THE CIVIL WAR—*Continued.*

NAMES.	Reg.	Page.	Remarks.
Quinn, James	4	192	
Quinn, John	4	192	Deserted.
Quinn, John	10	544	Died Wds., June 7, '64.
Quinn, Michael	11	588	
Quinn, Patrick	4	192	Deserted.
Quint, Isaac	10	544	Wounded.
Ramsay, William	7	388	Wd. Died July 2, '64.
Ramsay, William H.	3	139	
Rand, Charles J.	1 L. B.	902	
Rand, Lucius H.	1	17	
Rand, Perley B.	1	17	
Rand, Perley B.	4	192	
Rand, Perley B.	4	192	
Rand, William T.	1	17	
Randall, George W.	9	496	Deserted.
Randall, Noah M.	1 H. A.	951	
Randlett, Thomas	1 L. B.	902	
Raney, Thomas	28	1072	(28) Mass. Deserted.
Randolph, Joseph	1 V. C.	880	
Rawlston, James	9	496	Deserted.
Ray, Alexander H.	2	1072	(2) Mass. Deserted.
Ray, George H.	N. G.	994	
Ray, John	10	544	
Ray, Philip	8	442	Deserted.
Raymond, Joseph	1	18	
Raymond, Mortimer E.	10	544	Wd. Died June 15, '64.
Reagan, Thomas	7	389	
Reagan, Thomas	V.R.C.	1012	
Reagan, Patrick	8	442	Wounded.
Reagan, Patrick	8	442	Died wds., June 20, '63.
Rearden, Dennis W.	1 H. A.	951	
Reardon, Michael	4	192	Deserted.
Reardon, Timothy	4	192	Died May 1, '65.
Redfield, Frank H.	N. G.	994	
Reed, Alonzo	8	442	Wounded.
Reed, Alonzo	V.R.C.	1012	
Reed, Charles H.	1	18	
Reed, Charles H.	4	192	
Reed, Elbridge	8	442	Wounded.
Reed, Elbridge	V.R.C.	1012	

NAMES.	Reg.	Page.	Remarks.
Reed, George T.	62	1070	(62) Mass.
Reeves, Francis	1 L. B.	902	
Reimann, Raphael	12	637	Deserted.
Remert, George F.	1	18	
Reynolds, Edward	3	140	Killed Oct. 13, '64.
Reynolds, Edmund T.	1	18	
Reynolds, Newton	1 V. C.	841	
Reynolds, Thomas	18	821	
Reynolds, William H.	4	192	
Reynolds, William H.	4	192	
Rhodes, Thomas	8	442	Deserted.
Richards, James	1 H. A.	952	
Richards, John	C. T.	1023	
Richards, John E.	2	79	
Richards, Lucien B.	1 L. B.	902	
Richards, Robert	1	18	
Richards, Walter J.	3	140	
Richards, Walter J.	3	140	
Richardson, Carlton C.	4	193	
Richardson, Edwin P.	Navy.	1158	
Richardson, Henry K.	4	193	Killed May 16, '64.
Richardson, Horace L.	1 H. A.	952	
Richardson, Hugh R.	1 V. C.	880	Dishon. discharged.
Richardson, Martin V.B.	1	18	
Richardson, Martin V.B.	4	193	
Richardson, Moses	11	589	Wounded.
Ricker, John E.	N. G.	994	
Ridley, David L.	10	544	
Riley, John W.	2	79	Deserted.
Riley, Michael	7	389	Died Wds., Aug 9, '63.
Riley, Terrence	2	79	Deserted to the enemy.
Riley, Thomas	2	79	Wounded.
Ringlar, George W.	1	18	
Riordan, John	10	544	Wounded.
Rivers, John C.	Navy.	1159	
Roach, James C.	3	140	
Robbins, Henry T.	7	390	
Roberts, Andrew J.	1 V. C.	881	
Roberts, Charles	3	140	Deserted.
Roberts, Isaac L.	1 L. B.	902	

MANCHESTER MEN IN THE CIVIL WAR—*Continued.*

NAMES.	Reg.	Page.	Remarks.
Roberts, Orsino	2	80	
Roberts, William W.	1 L. B.	902	Died Dec. 25, '63.
Robie, George Frank	7	390	
Robie, George Frank	7	390	
Robie, John F. P.	8	443	
Robie. John F. P.	8	443	
Robinson, Albert B.	2	80	Wounded.
Robinson, Albert B.	1 H. A.	952	
Robinson, Frank O.	2	80	Killed Aug. 29, '62.
Robinson, George W.	4	193	
Robinson, James	10	545	Deserted.
Robinson, James H.	1 V. C.	881	
Robinson, John H.	8	443	Deserted.
Robinson, Peter	18	822	Deserted.
Robinson, Thomas	3	141	Wounded.
Robinson, Thomas	8	443	Deserted.
Robinson, William E.	4	193	
Robinson, William E.	V.R.C.	1012	
Roby, Joseph	7	390	Died Wds., Feb. 28, '64.
Rochester, Robert	7	390	
Rogers, Albert E.	1	18	
Rogers, Thomas H.	8	444	
Rogers, Thomas H.	8	444	
Rollins, Daniel W.	1	18	
Rollins, Daniel W.	4	193	
Rooney, James	1	18	
Ross, Alexander	5	264	Deserted.
Ross, Edwin J. A.	1 H. A.	953	
Rounds, John F.	18	822	
Rourke, Timothy	8	444	
Rourke, William	8	444	
Rowe, Alfred	7	390	
Rowe, Andrew J.	7	390	
Rowe, Andrew J.	V.R.C.	1013	
Rowe, Charles E.	8	444	Wounded.
Rowell, Charles A.	7	390	
Rowell, Charles A.	7	390	
Rumann, Louis	1 V. C.	881	
Runnals, Dana	4	194	
Runnals, Dana	4	194	

MANCHESTER MEN IN THE CIVIL WAR—*Continued.*

Names.	Reg.	Page.	Remarks.
Runnals, George A.	4	194	Wounded.
Russell, Barnabas B.	8	444	
Russell, Barnabas B.	8	444	
Russell, Daniel S.	4	194	
Russell, Warren I.	7	391	
Ryan, John J.	18	822	Deserted.[tenceG.C.M.
Ryan, William	10	545	Dis. discharged by sen-
Sage, Thomas	2	81	Died Oct. 17, '62.
Sanborn, Abram S.	4	194	Died Sept. 3, '62.
Sanborn, Charles H.	1	19	
Sanborn, Drew A.	9	499	
Sanborn, Drew A.	9	499	
Sanborn, Henry M.	10	545	
Sanborn, Sidney F.	M.G.	997	
Sanborn, Wheelock	2	1075	(2) Mass. Wounded.
Sanborn, William H.	4	194	
Sanborn, William H.	4	194	
Sargent, Albert F.	11	591	
Sargent, Arthur G.	1	19	
Sargent, Charles E.	10	546	
Sargent, Charles G.	2	82	Deserted.
Sargent, George H.	2	82	Wounded.
Sargent, Henry O.	9	987	
Sargent, James F.	1 L. B.	902	Wounded.
Sargent, John B.	10	546	
Sargent, John L.	1 L. B.	902	
Sargent, John L.	1 L. B.	902	
Sargent, Jeremiah A.	V.R.C.	1013	
Sargent, Larkin	4	194	
Sargent, Larkin	V.R.C.	1013	
Saunders, John H.	3	141	
Savage, Michael	8	445	
Sawtell, Edmond M.	7	391	Died Wds., Mar. 25,'64.
Sawyer, George W.	1 H.A.	954	
Sawyer, Myron A.	8	445	Wd. Died May 25, '64.
Sawyer, Zara	10	546	
Scanlin, Edwin	7	391	Wounded.
Schoopmeyer, Edward	5	266	
Schuyler, Benjamin	8	445	
Schwenke, Henry	2	82	

MANCHESTER MEN IN THE CIVIL WAR—*Continued.*

NAMES.	Reg.	Page.	Remarks.
Schwartz, Solomon	12	640	Wounded.
Schellenberg, Anton	7	391	
Searls, Loammi	11	592	Wounded.
Seaver, Robert A.	4	195	
Selingham, Frank W.	3	142	
Senter, James	8	445	
Senter, James	8	445	Died Wds., June 15, '64.
Senter, Samuel	7	391	
Shanley, James H.	9	500	Died April 24, '64.
Sharp, Joseph*	12	640	Shot for des., Feb.9,'65.
Shattuck, Amos B.	11	592	Died Wds., Dec. 17, '62.
Shaughnesey, Michael	4	195	
Shaughnesey, Michael	4	195	
Shay, Cornelius	28	1076	(28) Mass. Wounded.
Shea, John	4	195	Wd. severely, left on
Shea, John, 2d	8	446	[the field.
Shea, Martin	8	446	Deserted.
Shea, Michael	8	446	Died July 20, '62.
Shea, Patrick	8	446	Wounded.
Shea, William	8	446	Died Nov. 16, '62.
Shebassot, John	8	446	Deserted.
Sheedy, Roger	10	546	Wounded.
Sheehan, Edward	3	142	
Sheehan, Edward	3	142	Wounded.
Sheehan, Jeremiah	18	823	Deserted.
Sheehan, Jeremiah	17	1076	(17) Mass.
Sheehan, Eneas	8	446	
Sheehan, Jeremiah D.	10	546	
Sheehan, Jeremiah D.	V.R.C.	1013	
Shemenway, Alfred B.	7	392	
Shepard, George A.	1 L. B.	902	
Shepard, George A.	1 L. B.	902	
Shepherd, Charles H.	1 L. B.	902	
Shepherd, Levi B.	1	19	
Shepherd, Levi B.	1 L. B.	902	
Sherburn, Benjamin F.	M. G.	997	
Sherburne, Laroy D.	2	83	
Sherer, Charles G.	7	392	
Sherer, William	4	195	Died Nov. 1, '61.
Sheridan, Francis	3	142	Wounded. Deserted.

* Not a citizen, credited to Manchester.

MANCHESTER MEN IN THE CIVIL WAR—*Continued.*

NAMES.	Reg.	Page.	Remarks.
Sherlock, Antoney	3	142	
Shibin, John	14	724	
Sholes, Albert E.	2	83	
Sholes, Albert E.	2	83	Wounded.
Shortell, John	3	142	Deserted.
Shoughra, Timothy	7	392	
Shoughra, Timothy	V.R.C.	1013	
Shultz, George	2	83	
Sias, Edwin R.	1 L. B.	902	
Sibley, Roswell T.	18	446	
Silloway, Orrin S.	1 L. B.	902	
Silloway, Orrin S.	1 L. B.	902	
Silver, John O.	7	392	
Simonds, John S.	12	1076	(12) Mass. Wounded.
Simons, Alfred G.	10	549	
Simons, Hiram A.	4	195	
Simmons, Albion R.	2	83	
Simmons, Albion R.	2	83	
Simmons, Volney T.	3	142	
Simpson, Alexander	1 L. B.	902	
Sinery, James	8	446	Deserted.
Sleeper, Levi H., Jr.	2	84	
Sleeper, Levi H., Jr.	1 H. A.	955	
Sloan, Henry A.	1 L. B.	902	
Sloden, James	3	143	Died Aug. 12, '62.
Smiley, Charles H.	2	84	Killed Aug. 29, '62.
Smiley, Stephen J.	2	84	
Smith, Alvin R.	2	84	
Smith, Benjamin W.	4	196	
Smith, Charles	2	84	Deserted.
Smith, Charles A.	N. G.	994	
Smith, Charles F.	8	446	
Smith, Charles F.	8	446	
Smith, Charles H.	11	592	Wounded.
Smith, Charles W.	10	547	Wounded.
Smith, Chauncey H.	4	196	Died Nov. 24, '63.
Smith, Curtis	1	20	
Smith, Curtis	8	446	
Smith, Curtis	8	446	Wounded.
Smith, Daniel A., Jr.	Navy.	1164	

MANCHESTER MEN IN THE CIVIL WAR—*Continued.*

Names.	Reg.	Page.	Remarks.
Smith, Donald	3	143	
Smith, Donald	3	143	
Smith, Edward	2	84	Deserted.
Smith, Edwin O.	10	547	Deserted.
Smith, George	7	393	
Smith, George E.	7	393	Died Oct. 9, '63.
Smith, Gilman M.	11	593	Died Feb. 10, '64.
Smith, Henry M.	1	20	
Smith, Howard P.	M. G.	997	
Smith, James	18	824	Deserted.
Smith, James	Navy.	1165	
Smith, James	Navy.	1165	Deserted.
Smith, James	3	143	Died Nov. 13, '62.
Smith, John	4	196	
Smith, John	4	196	Deserted.
Smith, John	2	85	Died Wds., July 10,'64.
Smith, John	28	1077	(28) Mass.
Smith, John	8	447	Wounded.
Smith, John	V.R.C.	1013	
Smith, John	8	447	
Smith, John	11	593	
Smith, John	12	641	Wounded.
Smith, John	Navy.	1165	
Smith, John P.	4	196	Died Dec. 30, '61.
Smith, Lewis J.	1 H. A.	955	
Smith, Lewis J.	M. G.	997	
Smith, Luther M.	11	593	Died Wds., Nov. 26, '64.
Smith, Merrick E.	M. G.	997	
Smith, Peter	3	143	Died Wds., Aug. 30, '64
Smith, Richard	4	196	
Smith, Richard	4	196	
Smith, Reuben V. G.	11	593	
Smith, Thomas	5	268	Deserted,
Smith, Thomas	2	85	
Smith, Thomas, 2d.	3	144	Killed Oct. 7, '64.
Smith, Walter	1 H. A.	955	
Smith, William	7	393	
Smith, William	8	447	
Smith, William	V.R.C.	1013	
Smith, William	2	85	

MANCHESTER MEN IN THE CIVIL WAR—*Continued.*

NAMES.	Reg.	Page.	Remarks.
Smith, William	1 V. C.	884	
Snow, Joseph T.	4	197	
Snow, Joseph T.	V.R.C.	1013	
Sock, Peter	18	824	Deserted.
Solen, Thomas. 2d	10	547	Wounded.
Sorensen, Charles	12	641	
Soule, Gustavus	1 L. B.	902	
Soule, Gustavus	1 L. B.	902	
Spaulding, Benjamin	4	197	
Spaulding, George E.	1 V. C.	884	
Spaulding, Fernando C.	4	197	Died Nov. 7, '64.
Spear, Joseph A.	8	447	
Spear, Robert	7	394	
Spelan, Jeremiah	4	197	Wounded.
Spelan, Jeremiah	4	197	Died March 16, '65.
Spicer, Christian	1	20	
Sprague, William	3	144	Wounded. Deserted.
Squire, Noble	1	20	
Squires, Hiram C.	3	144	
Stanley, Harry	8	447	Deserted.
Stanton, George	5	269	Killed April 7, '65.
Stanton, Martin J.*	4	197	Killed March 16, '62.
Stark, Daniel F.	10	547	
Stark, William G.	2	86	
Stark, William G.	2	86	
Stead, James W.	3	144	Died Wds., July 14, '64.
Stearns, Albert C.	1 L. B.	902	
Stearns, Charles H.	N. G.	994	
Stearns, Gilman	1 L. B.	902	
Stearns, Hiram	1 V. C.	843	Wounded.
Stearns, William E.	15·	757	
Stearns, William K.	10	548	
Stearns, William	15	757	
Steele, William	2	86	
Stenger, Augustus	4	197	Deserted.
Stephens, Samuel	5	269	
Stetson, James	5	270	Died Jan. 4, '64.
Stevens, Albert H.	3	144	
Stevens, Albert H.	3	144	Wounded.
Stevens, Charles W.	2 R. S.	981	

*In a riot at Jacksonville, Florida.

MANCHESTER MEN IN THE CIVIL WAR—*Continued.*

NAMES.	Reg.	Page.	Remarks.
Stevens, Benjamin	11	594	
Stevens, Daniel	8	448	
Stevens, David P.	M. G.	997	
Stevens, David P.	1 H. A.	956	Died June 14, '65.
Stevens, Edwin R.	8	448	
Stevens, Enoch C.	4	197	
Stevens, Enoch C.	V R.C.	1014	
Stevens, Everett	1 H. A.	956	Died Oct. 16, '64.
Stevens, George W.	4	197	
Stevens, George W.	4	197	
Stevens, Horatio N.	2	87	
Stevens, Horatio N.	4	197	
Stevens, Horatio N.	5	270	Died July 12, '64.
Stevens, Monroe	4	197	
Stevens, Monroe	4	197	
Stevens, Reuben F.	2	87	
Stevens, William O.	11	594	
Stewart, Frank W.	2	1079	(2) Mass.
Stewart, John	4	197	Died Nov. 22, '64.
Stewart, Robert	1 H. A.	956	
Stiles, George D.	4	197	
Stoddard, Asahel	4	198	
Stokes, John F.	3	144	
Stokes, John F.	3	144	Wounded.
Stokes, Orrin N. B.	4	198	
Stokes, Orrin N. B.	N. G.	994	
Stokes, Septimus	10	548	
Stone, Cornelius H.	5	270	Wounded.
Stone, Cornelius H.	5	270	
Stone, Judson	7	395	Died Feb. 17, '64.
Stone, Ralph	8	448	
Stoughton, Andrew W.	1 H. A.	956	Died Nov. 22, '64.
Strain, Charles E.	10	548	Died Jan. 14, '63.
Strain, Cornelius W.	10	548	
Straw, William H.	2	88	
Strong, William	8	448	Deserted.
Stuart, Charles	V.R.C.	1014	Deserted.
Stuart, George H.	4	198	Wounded.
Stuart, George H.	4	198	Died Sept. 11, '64.
Stuart, Zachariah B.	18	824	

Names.	Reg.	Page.	Remarks.
Sturtevant, Elwin	7	395	
Sturtevant, Elwin	7	395	
Sturtevant, Elwin	Navy.	1168	
Sughrue, Patrick	10	548	
Sullivan, Cornelius C.	4	198	
Sullivan, Cornelius C.	4	198	Deserted.
Sullivan, Daniel	4	198	
Sullivan, Daniel	4	198	
Sullivan, Dennis	10	548	
Sullivan, Dennis	1	1079	(1) R. I. Deserted.
Sullivan, Edson	1 H. A.	957	
Sullivan, James	3	144	
Sullivan, James	3	144	Wounded.
Sullivan, James	8	448	
Sullivan, James	8	448	Drowned, July 14, '64.
Sullivan, James	Navy.	1169	Deserted.
Sullivan, John	8	448	
Sullivan, John	10	548	
Sullivan, John	Navy.	1169	Deserted.
Sullivan, John, 2d	8	448	Died Wds., Apr. 9, '64.
Sullivan, Michael	8	448	Deserted.
Sullivan, Michael	8	448	Wounded.
Sullivan, Michael	8	448	Wounded.
Sullivan, Michael	10	548	Died Wds., Aug. 27,'64.
Sullivan, Michael	17	1079	(17) Mass.
Sullivan, Owen	10	548	
Sullivan, Patrick	8	449	Died Oct. 19, '64.
Sullivan, Patrick	8	449	Deserted.
Sullivan, Patrick	Navy.	1169	
Sullivan, Patrick	18	824	
Sullivan, Patrick, Jr.	8	449	Deserted.
Sullivan, William	4	198	
Sullivan, William	4	198	Killed May 16, '64.
Summerfield, Walter	5	271	Deserted to the enemy.
Summers, Henry H.	7	395	
Summers, William	2	88	
Summers, William	V.R.C.	1014	
Sutton, William	12	642	
Swaine, George E.	1 H. A.	957	
Swaine, George E.	M. G.	997	

MANCHESTER MEN IN THE CIVIL WAR—*Continued.*

Names.	Reg.	Page.	Remarks.
Swain, Josiah S.	2	88	
Sweatt, William W.	1 H.A.	957	
Swett, Nathaniel F.	2	88	
Swinburn, George W.	N. G.	994	
Swiney, Robert*	8	449	Died April 9, '63.
Sylvester, Leander G.	1 L. B.	903	
Syms, Ruel S.	3	145	
Taber, Charles L.	2	88	Wounded.
Taber, Charles L.	1 L. B.	903	
Taber, Frank W.	1 L. B.	903	
Taber, Orrin	1 L. B.	903	
Taffe, Matthew	8	449	Wounded.
Taft, John	2	88	
Tallant, Eben M.	1	20	
Tallin, Joseph	2	88	Deserted.
Taplin, Lewis E.	1 V. C.	843	
Tasker, Albert P.	1 V. C.	843	
Taylor, Charles	5	272	
Taylor, George W.	1 H.A.	957	
Taylor, Ira	12	643	Deserted.
Taylor, Thomas	10	549	Deserted.
Teahan, Timothy	10	549	Deserted.
Tebbitts, Hanson	10	549	
Tehan, Dennis	4	199	
Tennant, Matthew P.	9	503	{March 15, '65.
Thayer, George W. A.	24		(24) New York. !Died
Thomas, George S.	3	145	Deserted.
Thomas, William H.	4	199	Deserted.
Thompson, Charles H.	10	549	Deserted.
Thompson, Henry	8	449	Wounded.
Thompson, Henry	8	449	
Thompson, Jehiel M.	8	449	
Thompson, Jehiel M.	8	449	Died Feb. 22, '65.
Thompson, James	10	549	Deserted.
Thompson, John	2	89	
Thompson, John	5	273	Wounded. Deserted.
Thompson, William R.	7	396	Deserted.
Thomson, Thomas	3	145	Wounded.
Thomson, Thomas	U.S.V.	145	
Thornton, Daniel	Navy.	1190	Deserted.

*Committed suicide, supposed insane.

MANCHESTER MEN IN THE CIVIL WAR—*Continued*

NAMES.	Reg.	Page.	Remarks.
Thornton, John	8	449	
Thunblom, Reinhold T.	4	199	
Thurber, Freeman N.	3	145	Wounded.
Tibbetts, Collins P.	3	145	
Tibbetts, Collins P.	3	145	
Tillotson, Edward M.	1 H. A.	958	
Tillotson, Edward M.	N. G.	994	
Tilton, Albert	1	21	
Tilton, Nathan B.	1 L. B.	903	
Tilton, Nathan B.	1 L. B.	903	
Tilton, William H.	2	90	
Tobie, Addison W.	1	21	
Tobie, Addison W.	4	200	
Tobie, Addison W.	17	799	
Tobie, Irving D.	15	758	
Tobin, Richard	1 V. C.	886	Deserted.
Tobin, Stephen	8	450	Died Dec. 28, '62.
Todd, William	3	145	
Todd, William	3	145	Wounded.
Tomes, Henry	12	643	
Tompkins, Henry D.	4	200	
Tonrey, Thomas	3	145	
Toole, Martin	10	549	
Towal, Thomas	8	450	Deserted.
Town, Solomon	18	825	
Towne, Russell	10	549	
Towns, Allison	6	341	
Towns, James B. F.	3	146	
Towns, James B. F.	3	146	
Tracy, James	2	90	
Travis, John B.	2	90	Deserted.
Trumbel, Gustine M.	1	21	
Trumbull, Thomas C.	10	550	
Tuck, George S.	4	200	Died April 1, '65.
Tucker, Franklin K.	2	90	Wounded.
Tucker, Franklin K.	V.R.C.	1014	Deserted.
Tufts, Charles H.	11	596	
Tulley, Owen	4	200	Wounded.
Tulley, Owen	4	200	
Tuttle, Charles D.	2	91	

NAMES.	Reg.	Page.	Remarks.
Tuttle, Charles D.	2	91	Wounded.
Tuttle, Edwin N.	18	825	
Tuttle, Edwin N.	N. G.	994	
Tuttle, Marcus M.	2	91	
Tuttle, Marcus M.	8	450	
Tuttle, Marcus M.	11	1082	(11) Mass.
Tuttle, Nathaniel A.	18	825	
Tuttle, Nathaniel A.	N. G.	994	
Twichell, Evi P.	1 L. B.	903	
Twichell, Evi P.	1 L. B.	903	
Twombly, Henry W.	1 H. A.	959	
Tyson, Tye	6	341	Died Dec. 7, '64.
Underhill, William B.	1	21	
Underhill, William B.	1 L. B.	903	
Untiet, Barnard	10	550	Wounded.
Varnum, George W.	1 L. B.	903	
Varnum, George W.	V.R.C.	1014	
Vezeay, Walter	8	450	Deserted.
Vickery, Charles	2	91	Died Wds., July 11,'63.
Vincent, Richard	2	91	
Vincent, Richard	2	91	Died May 20, '65.
Vincent, Rupert	3	146	Died Dec. 5, '64.
Von Strombeck, Carlos	3	1082	(3) Mass. Deserted.
Vosburg, Charles N.	2	91	
Vose, Joshua S.	1 V. C.	886	
Vradenburg, Solomon	8	450	
Wadleigh, John	1 L. B.	903	Wounded.
Waldan, Ernest F.	2	92	Wounded.
Walker, Charles H.	2	1082	(2) Mass.
Walker, David	7	397	Deserted.
Walker, James P.	4	200	
Walker, James W.	12	1082	(12) Mass. Deserted.
Walker, Joseph E.	1 H. A.	959	
Wall, William H.	10	550	
Wallace, Edward	7	397	
Wallace, James M.	1 H. A.	959	
Wallace, Joseph H.	3	146	
Wallace, Joseph H.	9	505	Died Oct. 19, '63.
Wallace, John A.	2	1083	(2) Mass.
Wallace, Luther E.	1 L. B.	903	

MANCHESTER MEN IN THE CIVIL WAR—*Continued.*

NAMES.	Reg.	Page.	Remarks.
Wallace, Patrick	7	397	Died Aug. 11, '62.
Wallace, Selwin B.	1 H. A.	959	
Wallace, Silas R.	14	728	
Wallace, William J.	12	644	Deserted.
Walley, Henry	10	550	Deserted.
Walsh, Dennis	4	200	
Walsh, Dennis	4	200	Wounded.
Walsh, John	4	201	
Walsh, John	8	450	
Walsh, Patrick	8	450	
Walsh, Patrick	V.R.C.	1014	
Walsh, Patrick	10	550	
Walsh, Sylvester S.	1 H. A.	959	
Walsh, Sylvester S.	M. G.	997	
Ward, Charles	10	550	
Ward, John	10	550	
Ward, Theodore T.	4	201	
Warden, Frank	10	550	Deserted.
Wardmann, Carlos	12	644	
Warren, Alonzo F.	N. G.	994	
Warren, Henry J.	8	451	Deserted.
Warren, Joseph	4	201	
Warren, Phillip	12	645	Deserted.
Warren, William	14	729	
Wasley, Frank C.	2	92	Wounded.
Wasley, Frazer A.	10	550	
Wason, Elbridge	M. G.	997	
Watson, Lorenzo D.	12	645	
Waugh, William	8	451	
Way, Charles	18	826	
Weaver, George	1	22	
Weaver, George	7	398	
Weaver, James	7	398	Died Nov. 7, '64.
Webster, Caius C.	10	551	
Webster, David O.	7	398	
Webster, George H.	3	147	
Webster, George H.	3	147	
Webster, Henry J.	1 V. C.	887	
Webster, John W.	16	1083	(16) Maine.
Webster, Joshua B.	4	201	

MANCHESTER MEN IN THE CIVIL WAR—*Continued.*

NAMES.	Reg.	Page.	Remarks.
Webster, Nahum A.	1 H. A.	959	
Webster, Nathaniel	9	506	
Webster, Sylvester F.	1 L. B.	903	
Webster, William A.	9	506	
Webster, William H.	4	201	
Webster, William H.	4	201	
Weed, Harvey M.	4	201	
Weinhold, Ernest	1	22	
Welden, William	12	645	
Welch, Benjamin	4	201	
Welch, Charles	9	507	Died Jan. 28, '64.
Welch, James	3	147	
Welch, James	3	147	
Welch, James	4	201	
Welch, James	4	201	Wounded.
Welch, James	8	451	
Welch, Stephen	3	147	
Welch, Thomas	1	22	
Welch, Thomas	1 L. B.	903	Wounded.
Welch, Thomas	1 L. B.	903	
Welch, Thomas	2	1083	(2) Mass.
Welch, Thomas	2	1083	(2) Mass. Wounded.
Wells, Clinton P.	7	398	
Wells, Daniel A.	1 H. A.	960	
Wells, George W.	1	22	
Wells, Gustavus B.	18	826	
Welpley, William	9	507	
Welsh, Patrick	3	147	
Wentworth, Andrew J.	10	551	Wounded.
Wenz, Charles	1 L. B.	903	
Weerman, Charles	M. G.	997	
Wescott, Gustine M.	9	507	Wounded.
Wescott, Gustine M.	V.R.C.	1014	
Weston, Samuel	1	22	
Weston, Samuel	8	451	
Wheeler, Alfred	10	551	
Wheeler, George N.	10	551	Died Aug. 24, '64.
Whelston, Thomas	4	202	Died Wds., Aug. 8, '64.
Whidden, William	2	93	Wounded.
Whipple, Clark B.	7	399	

NAMES.	Reg.	Page.	Remarks.
White, Augustus	8	451	Deserted.
White, Bernard	10	551	Died April 3, '65.
White, Charles	6	343	
White, Charles A.	3	1084	(3) Mass.
White, Charles A.	3	148	Wounded.
White, Charles A.	U.S.V.	148	
White, Edward K.	18	826	
White, George A.	9	1084	(9) Mass.
White, George F.	18	826	
White, Horace J.	7	399	Wounded.
White, James	4	202	
White, John	7	399	Wounded.
White, John	7	399	Wounded.
White, John	8	451	
White, John	11	598	
White, John	11	598	
White, Joseph W.	7	399	Killed July 18, '63.
White, Leander	3	148	Wounded.
White, Matthew B.	1 H.A.	960	
White, William W.	10	551	Deserted.
Whitford, Edwin	4	202	
Whitcher, Roland C.	5	277	Wounded.
Whiting, Charles M.	4	202	
Whiting, Charles M.	4	202	Wounded.
Whitney, Daniel D.	11	598	
Whitney, John	3	148	Killed May 16, '64.
Whittaker, Samuel	3	148	Wounded.
Whittemore, Chas. F.	1 H.A.	961	
Whittemore, Chas. F.	N.G.	994	
Whitten, John R.	3	148	
Whittier, Samuel J.	1 L.B.	903	
Whittle, Thomas J.	1 L.B.	903	
Whittle, Thomas J.	2 H.A.	918	
Wiggin, Alvin S.	2	94	
Wiggin, Thomas J.	14	730	
Wiley, Charles W.	10	551	
Wiley, Charles W.	V.R.C.	1015	
Willey, Francis B.	4	203	Deserted.
Willey, Henry M.	9	508	Died Aug. 20, '63.
Willey, John W.	1 H.A.	961	

MANCHESTER MEN IN THE CIVIL WAR—*Continued.*

NAMES.	Reg.	Page.	Remarks.
Willard, John B.	8	452	Deserted.
Wilkins, Ira Gardner	11	598	Wounded.
Wilkins, William W.	2	94	
Wilkins, William W.	Navy.	1177	
Williams, Charles	8	452	
Williams, Charles E.	12	646	Deserted.
Williams, Charles H.	4	203	
Williams, Charles H.	4	203	Wounded.
Williams, Edson	1 V. C.	844	
Williams, Edson	V.R.C.	1015	
Williams, George P.	2	94	
Williams, George W.	4	203	
Williams, George W.	4	203	
Williams, Hanson T.	3	149	Killed June 16, '62.
Williams, Isaac	C. T.	1026	
Williams, Jackson	1	1086	(1) Mass.
Williams, James	7	399	
Williams, John	2	95	
Williams, John	8	452	Deserted.
Williams, John	8	452	
Williams, William P.	10	552	Wounded. Deserted.
Williamson, Peter	4	203	
Wilson, Adam D.	C. T.	1026	
Wilson, Alvah D.	4	203	
Wilson, Charles	18	827	
Wilson, Charles H.	1 V. C.	844	
Wilson, Clark E.	4	203	
Wilson, David A.	1 H. A.	961	
Wilson, David F.	1 V. C.	844	
Wilson, David F.	1 V. C.	844	
Wilson, Ebenezer	1 V. C.	844	Wounded.
Wilson, Frank	12	646	
Wilson, James	3	149	
Wilson, James	8	452	Deserted.
Wilson, John	3	1086	(3) Mass. Deserted.
Wilson, Stephen M.	14	731	
Wing, Edward J.	1 H. A.	961	
Wing, Edward J.	M. G.	997	
Wing, Harrison B.	3	150	
Wingate, Charles W.	1 H. A.	961	

NAMES.	Reg.	Page.	Remarks.
Witham, Amos R.	3	150	Wounded.
Wolfendale, William	3	150	
Wood, Charles	7	400	
Wood, William W.	2	95	
Woods, Samuel	2	95	
Woods, Patrick	3	150	Wounded.
Woodburn, George A.	3	150	Wounded.
Woodburn, George A.	3	150	Killed Aug. 16, '64.
Woodbury, Daniel K.	11	600	Killed May 12, '64.
Woodbury, Roger W.	3	150	Wounded.
Woodbridge, Wm. O.	4	204	Died Wds., June 25, '64.
Worthen, Frederick S.	1 L. B.	993	
Wooster, John C.	10	552	Wounded.
Wright, Charles B.	2	96	Deserted.
Wright, Ira E.	11	600	
Wyman, Albion	16	789	
Wyman, Alonzo	5	280	Deserted.
Wyman, Arnold	1 V. C.	845	Wounded.
Wyman, Daniel	8	453	
Wyman, Edson	4	205	
Wyman, Edson	4	205	
Wyman, Emery	4	205	Wounded.
Wyman, Edward A.	2 H. A.	918	
Wyman, George	4	205	
Wyman, George H.	10	552	Wd. Died Feb. 6, '65.
Wyman, James	4	205	
Wyman, James	4	205	
Wyman, Lyman	4	205	
Wyman, Woodbury	4	205	
Wyman, Woodbury	4	205	
Yates, Jerome	U.S.A.	1087	
Yeaton, William H.	1	23	
York, Francis	1 H. A.	962	
York, Francis	7	1087	(7) Rhode Island.
Young, Albert A.	2	1087	(2) Mass. Deserted.
Young, Albert A. M. L.	8	453	
Young, Albert P.	1 H. A.	911	
Young, Charles E.	1 L. B.	903	
Young, Charles E.	1 L. B.	903	
Young, Morrill N.	1 L. B.	903	
Young, William Q.	1 H. A.	962	

STATE SERVICE.

www.ingramcontent.com/pod-product-compliance
Lightning Source LLC
Chambersburg PA
CBHW020544270326
41927CB00006B/709